Eat, Fish
and Be Happy

Give a man a fish and he will eat for a day. Teach him how to fish and he will sit in a boat and drink beer all day.

-Author Unknown

Additional recipes by
TJ Weston can be found
on his website and recipe blog at

www.westonfoodconsulting.com

Eat, Fish
and Be Happy

Salmon - and - Halibut

recipes to celebrate
the taste of
Alaska

Chef TJ Weston

Order this book online at www.trafford.com
or email orders@trafford.com

Most Trafford titles are also available at major online book retailers.

Printed in Victoria, BC, Canada.

ISBN: 978-1-4269-3158-1 (soft)
ISBN: 978-1-4269-3159-8 (hard)

Library of Congress Control Number: 2010905871

*Our mission is to efficiently provide the world's finest, most comprehensive book publishing
service, enabling every author to experience success. To find out how to publish your book, your
way, and have it available worldwide, visit us online at www.trafford.com*

Trafford rev. 5/26/2010

Trafford PUBLISHING®   www.trafford.com

North America & international
toll-free: 1 888 232 4444 (USA & Canada)
phone: 250 383 6864 ♦ fax: 812 355 4082

Thank you mom for the constant support,
to those who inspire and enjoy my cooking,
and especially Jessie and Tate; I Love You.

Contents

Asian Fish Cakes, Crab Dip, Pita Chips, Fresh Salsa, Halibut Ceviche, Reuben Dip, Salmon Dip, Salmon Lox, Salsa Verde, Seafood Cocktail Spicy Salmon Tartar, Warm Spinach Dip

Beef Chili, Broccoli Cheddar, Cheesy Potato, Clam Chowder, Coconut Fish Stew, Corn Chowder, Cream of Mushroom, Mexican Style Stew, Pozole, Split Pea, Southwest Chipotle Chicken, Tomato Soup, Alaskan Cioppino

Beet and Goat Cheese, Bacon Lettuce Tomato and Turkey, Tomato and Cucumber with Blue Cheese, Caesar, Chef, Ham 'n Swiss, Bacon Egg and Cheese, Reuben, Salami and Mozzarella, Simple Garden

Bacon Wrapped, Baked with Swiss and Mushrooms, Beer Battered, Broiled with Caramelized Onions, Buffalo, Coconut Fried, Drunken, Grilled with Citrus Butter, Herb Crusted, Sautéed with Capers and Tomatoes, Seared with Caper Cream, Simple Grilled, Sweet and Sour Stir Fry

Almond Crusted, Baked Cacciatore, Barbequed, Broiled with Lemon-Dill Butter, Cedar Plank, Cold Smoked, Crispy Fried, Grilled with Creamy Horseradish, Honey Mustard Glazed, Sesame Salmon, Simple Grilled, Slow Roasted Teriyaki, Tortilla Fried

Introduction

This book is more than just an assortment of recipes that I have created while cooking in Alaska, it is a collection of some of the best foods that I have had a lot of pleasure and success preparing at the fishing lodge over the years. It began as an attempt to organize all of my recipes, the one that were in my head, randomly scribbled on little notes, and even just the ideas that I had been playing with. I spent the winter months organizing and refining all of these until I had a crude book that I brought back with me the following summer. Now when a client asked for a recipe or wanted some suggestions for what to do with their fish when they got back home I could provide them with more than just a hand written copy of one of my recipes. The response to that first book was very positive so I continued updating and refining it until I got what I considered to be the very best of my Alaskan experiences. That is the book you are holding now.

This all began several years ago when a friend of mine that I had worked with in Los Angeles told me about a job he had landed for the summer. It would be in Alaska and as we talked more about it I became very intrigued. Soon I found myself on a plane headed to Sitka to work as the chef at a sport fishing lodge and will always remember the thrill that I felt as we descended through the clouds and the horizon came into view. I knew immediately that this place was extraordinary as my eyes wandered across the landscape from the mountains that were still capped in snow to the ocean that was both tranquil and aggressive at once. I had spent the last several years living in large cities and what lay before me now was a drastic change that I eagerly embraced.

The waters surrounding the island were home to some of the greatest seafood in the world ranging from wild salmon and halibut to cold water prawns and crab. Many restaurants across the country spend a lot of money to get fish flown in fresh from Alaska and now I could literally just go out and catch it myself, and I did. I have caught countless King Salmon and

Halibut over the years and never tire at the prospect of landing another one. To be able to catch it and cook it for dinner that evening amazed me and inspired the way that I would prepare and cook the fish. I developed an approach to cooking the fish that would accentuate its wonderful qualities and not mask them or take anything away from the dish. I knew how fortunate that I was to have access to such amazing fish and to have the opportunity to cook it every day. Seven days a week for four and a half months I would prepare dinner that would include a salmon and halibut dish, as well as a meat, a few side items, fresh bread and homemade desserts. It was my job to feed the clients and make sure that they ate well, after dinner I would talk to them and listen to their feedback to learn what I needed to improve upon or do differently. It was a lot of work but it was also a wonderful experience that taught me so much and provided such amazing opportunities that I will forever remember my time in Alaska very fondly.

APPETIZERS

Whether the start of a meal or served by themselves at a party, appetizers should be pleasurable and exciting. There are no limits to what can be offered from simple dips to elaborate bite sized entrees because as long as they are fun and creative they will be enjoyed.

Asian Fish Cakes

Panko Bread Crumbs are a Japanese style found at most supermarkets but if unavailable regular bread crumbs will work just fine.

Ingredients

Leftover fish, coarsely flaked	2 cups
Panko Bread Crumbs	2 cups
Egg, lightly beaten	3 each
Cilantro leaves, chopped	2 tablespoons
Green Onion, white part only, chopped	1 tablespoon
Pickled Ginger, drained and chopped	1 tablespoon
Cumin, ground	1 teaspoon
Mayonnaise	2 tablespoons
Salt	2 teaspoons
White Pepper	1 teaspoon
Flour	2 cups
Sesame Seeds	2 tablespoons
Buttermilk	2 cups
Vegetable Oil	1 – 2 cups

Preparation

1. In a large bowl gently mix the fish, 2 tablespoons of bread crumbs, one egg, cilantro, green onion, pickled ginger, cumin, mayonnaise, salt, and white pepper. Mix just enough to combine everything then shape into six patties, each about 1" thick. Refrigerate.

2. Place the flour into a pie plate or shallow pan. Pour the buttermilk and remaining eggs into a second pan and mix well with a fork. Put the remaining breadcrumbs and sesame seeds into a third pan. Take a patty, and gently coat it in the flour and carefully pat off any excess, then dip into the buttermilk and drain any excess before coating with the bread crumbs. Place the breaded patty onto a plate and reshape as needed. Repeat with the remaining patties.

3. Add the vegetable oil to a large skillet until about ½" deep. Heat over medium to medium high heat until hot but not smoking. Add three patties and cook until golden brown on one side, about three minutes. Turn and finish cooking. Remove from pan and drain on paper towels.

4. Serve this with a little Chili Aioli (Pg. 171) spooned on top of each patty.

Crab Dip

Ingredients

Cream Cheese, softened	1 pound
Mayonnaise	8 ounces
Crab Meat	1 pound
Chives, minced	2 tablespoons
Dill, chopped	1 tablespoon
Lemon, juiced	1 each
Tabasco Sauce	½ teaspoon
Salt and White Pepper	to taste
Bread Crumbs	½ cup

Preparation

1. Preheat the oven to 350°

2. Mix the cream cheese and mayonnaise together in a bowl until smooth.

3. Fold in the crab meat, chives, dill, lemon juice, Tabasco, salt and white pepper. Taste for seasoning.

4. Put into a casserole dish and spread into an even layer. Sprinkle with the bread crumbs and bake until hot and bubbly, about 20 – 30 minutes.

5. Serve with pita chips (pg. 5), tortilla chips or toast points.

Chef TJ Weston

Pita Chips

Ingredients

Pita Bread, 6" rounds	5 each
Olive Oil	¼ cup
Garlic, chopped	1 tablespoon
Parsley, chopped	1 tablespoon
Salt and Black Pepper	to taste

Preparation

1. Preheat the oven to 400°

2. Cut the pita breads into six wedges each. Place in a large bowl.

3. Add the olive oil, garlic, and parsley. Season with salt and pepper and mix gently so as not to break the bread wedges.

4. Place onto a baking sheet in one layer and bake until golden brown and crispy. About 8 – 12 minutes.

Fresh Salsa

Ingredients

Roma Tomatoes, seeded and chopped	10 each
Onion, chopped	1 each
Jalapeno, seeded and chopped	1 each
Cilantro, chopped	1 bunch
Lime, juiced	3 each
Salt	to taste

Preparation

1. Mix everything together in a bowl, seasoning with salt as needed. Cover and refrigerate.

2. The trick to making this salsa is the smaller the ingredients are chopped, the tastier it will be. Using a food processor or electric chopper will make the salsa watery and soggy; cut all of the ingredients by hand with a sharp knife.

Halibut Ceviche

Fresh avocado makes a very nice addition to this, simply cut one or two into ¼ inch cubes and add with the tomatoes and onion.

Ingredients

Halibut, chopped	2 pounds
Lime, juiced	6 each
Roma Tomatoes, seeded and chopped	10 each
Onion, chopped	2 each
Jalapeno, seeded and chopped	1 each
Cilantro, chopped	1 bunch
Salt	to taste

Preparation

1. Mix the halibut and half of the lime juice together and refrigerate for three hours.

2. Drain the halibut and put into a bowl. Add all other ingredients and mix everything together, seasoning with salt as needed. Cover and refrigerate.

3. The trick to making this is the smaller the ingredients are chopped, the tastier it will be. Using a food processor or electric chopper will make the ceviche watery and soggy, cut all of the ingredients by hand with a sharp knife.

Reuben Dip

Ingredients

Cream Cheese, softened	1 pound
Mayonnaise	8 ounces
Pastrami, chopped	¼ pound
Sauerkraut, drained	¼ cup
Thousand Island Dressing	2 tablespoons
Swiss cheese, shredded	8 ounces

Preparation

1. Preheat the oven to 350°

2. Mix the cream cheese and mayonnaise together in a bowl until smooth.

3. Fold in the pastrami, sauerkraut, Thousand Island dressing and half of the cheese.

4. Put into a casserole dish and spread into an even layer. Sprinkle with the remaining cheese and bake until hot and bubbly, about 20 – 30 minutes.

5. Serve with pita chips (page 5), toasted rye bread or bagel chips.

Salmon Dip

Try substituting up to half of the cooked salmon with smoked salmon for an interesting twist.

Ingredients

Mayonnaise	1 cup
Sour Cream	1 cup
Lemon, juiced	1 each
Tomato Paste	2 teaspoons
Cooked Salmon, flaked	2 cups
Red Onion, minced	½ each
Capers, chopped	1 tablespoon
Parsley, chopped	1 tablespoon
Salt and White Pepper	to taste

Preparation

1. Mix the mayonnaise, sour cream, lemon juice, and tomato paste together in a large bowl.

2. Gently fold in the salmon, onion, capers, and parsley. Season with salt and white pepper.

3. Cover and refrigerate.

Salmon Lox

Ingredients

Salmon Filet, pin bones removed	1 each, about 5 pounds
Brown Sugar	10 cups
Kosher Salt	5 cups
Dill, dried	½ cup
Black Pepper	¼ cup

Preparation

1. In a large bowl mix together the sugar, salt, dill and pepper. Set aside.

2. Rinse the filet and pat dry with paper towels. Trim the filet as needed to make it fit into a large casserole dish or baking pan roughly 9" x 13".

3. Put a layer of the sugar mixture in the bottom of the pan about 1" thick. Add the fish skin side up and pack the pan with more sugar mixture including a ¼" layer on top of the skin.

4. Place another pan on top of the fish and weight it with a brick or other small items. Refrigerate for two full days.

5. Remove fish from pan and rinse the pan and fish off. Repeat the process, this time putting a ¼" of sugar on the bottom and the fish skin side down. Pack with more sugar, replace the pan and weight and refrigerate for another two days.

6. Remove fish from the pan and rinse under cold running water. Place on a rack skin side down and refrigerate uncovered overnight to allow it to dry. It will then be ready for slicing.

7. Serve this on top of bagels with cream cheese, crackers, or however you prefer. The lox can be smoked after drying in the refrigerator. Cold smoke the fish at 70° for 6 – 24 hours depending on the amount of flavor you want. Refrigerate overnight again before serving or wrapping and storing the fish.

Salsa Verde

This salsa is best when it is made the day before serving to allow all of the flavors to mellow out and blend together.

Ingredients

Tomatillos, peeled	2 pounds
Onion, ½" slices	2 each
Garlic, peeled	8 cloves
Jalapeno, seeded	1 each
Vegetable Oil	2 tablespoons
Salt	2 teaspoons
Cilantro, chopped	1 bunch
Lime, juiced	3 each

Preparation

1. Set the oven to broil and place the rack on the very top.

2. Mix the tomatillos, onion, garlic, jalapeno, oil and salt together in a bowl. Pour everything onto a pan and spread into an even layer. Broil until soft and slightly charred, about 7 minutes.

3. Remove from oven and allow to cool for a little while before pureeing in a blender until very smooth. Mix in the cilantro and lime juice, adjust seasoning as needed and refrigerate.

Seafood Cocktail

Ingredients

Large Shrimp, shells on	1 pound
King Crab Legs	1 pound
Dungeness Crabs	2 each
Salt	½ cup
Cocktail Sauce, page 173	1 cup
Lemons, cut into wedges	2 each

Preparation

1. Clean the Dungeness Crabs by removing the gills and splitting into quarters. Cut the King Crab Legs into 3 – 4" pieces. Set aside.

2. Add the salt to a large pot of water and bring to a boil over high heat. Once boiling, add the shrimp and cook just until they begin to float and are bright pink, about 4 minutes. Remove with a slotted spoon and place in a bowl. Cover with ice and refrigerate.

3. Bring the water back to a boil, add all of the crabs and legs, cover with a lid and return to a boil. Cook for fifteen minutes, remove and place in a bowl. Cover with ice and refrigerate until very cold.

4. Arrange all of the chilled seafood on a platter and garnish with the lemon wedges. Serve with the cocktail sauce on the side.

Spicy Salmon on Wonton Chips

Ingredients

Salmon, skinless 1/8" dice	2 cups
Green Onion, whites only, minced	2 tablespoons
Pickled Ginger, drained and minced	2 tablespoons
Soy Sauce	2 tablespoons
Wasabi Paste	1 tablespoon
Chili Aioli, page 171	¼ - ½ cup
Wontons, cut in half diagonally	12 each
Vegetable Oil	2 cups

Preparation

1. Mix the salmon, green onion, and ginger in a bowl and refrigerate.

2. In a small bowl mix the soy sauce and wasabi until smooth. Add to the salmon mixture with enough of the chili aioli so that everything is coated evenly and can hold its shape.

3. Heat the oil in a medium pot over medium to medium high heat. Once hot fry a few of the wontons until golden brown, stirring occasionally. Remove and drain on paper towels. Repeat until all of the chips have been fried.

4. Arrange the chips on a plate and top each one with a small amount of the salmon mixture.

Warm Spinach Dip

Ingredients

Frozen Spinach, chopped	10 ounces
Alfredo Sauce	10 ounces
Parmesan Cheese, grated	8 ounces
Mozzarella Cheese, shredded	4 ounces
Cream Cheese, softened	4 ounces
Garlic, chopped	2 cloves
Salt	2 teaspoon
White Pepper	1 teaspoon
Nutmeg	½ teaspoon

Preparation

1. Preheat oven to 375°

2. Thaw the spinach overnight in the refrigerator and then drain very well, making sure to squeeze out as much moisture as possible.

3. In a separate mixing bowl, combine the Alfredo sauce, parmesan cheese, mozzarella, salt, white pepper, and nutmeg. Mix well with a wooden spoon until no lumps remain.

4. Fold the spinach into the Alfredo mixture. Transfer to a shallow casserole dish and spread into an even layer and bake until hot and bubbly, about 20 – 30 minutes.

5. Serve with pita toast (page 5), tortilla chips or toasted rye bread.

SOUPS

I have always enjoyed making and eating soups all year long, from wintertime chili and hearty chowders to the light and refreshing broth soups of summertime. By themselves they can be a quick snack or begin a great meal and when paired with a couple pieces of fresh bread they make a hearty lunch or light supper. A great way to utilize leftovers or the perfect leftover for the next day, a pot of homemade soup is sure to satisfy.

Beef Chili

Ingredients

Olive Oil	1 tablespoon
Red Onions, chopped	2 each
Jalapeño, seeded and chopped	5 tablespoons
Garlic cloves, chopped	8 each
Ground Beef	2 1/2 pounds
Chili Powder	½ cup
Cumin, ground	3 tablespoons
Sweet Paprika	2 tablespoon
Canned Tomatoes, diced in juice	1 (28-ounce) can
Kidney Beans, drained	2 (15 1/4-ounce) cans
Beef Stock	2 cups
Salt	2 tablespoons
Black Pepper, ground	1 tablespoon

Preparation

1. Heat oil in heavy large pot over medium-high heat. Add onions; sauté until brown, about 6 minutes. Add jalapeños and garlic; sauté 1 minute. Add beef; sauté until brown, breaking up with back of fork, about 5 minutes.

2. Add chili powder, cumin, and paprika, then mix in tomatoes with juices, beans, and broth; bring to boil. Reduce heat and simmer until chili thickens and flavors blend, stirring occasionally, about 45 minutes. Skim any fat from surface of chili and season with the salt and black pepper.

Broccoli Cheddar

Ingredients

Butter, room temperature	6 tablespoons
Broccoli, fresh, stems and florets separated and chopped into bite size pieces	2 pounds
Onion, chopped	1 each
Garlic cloves, minced	2 each
Tarragon, dried	½ teaspoon
Chicken Stock	6 ½ cups
Heavy Cream	1 cup
Flour	3 tablespoons
Sharp Cheddar Cheese, grated	2 cups (packed)

Preparation

1. Melt butter in a heavy stock pot over medium high heat. Add broccoli stems and onion. Cook until onion is translucent, about 6 minutes. Add garlic and tarragon, cook for 1 minute. Stir in the flour and then add the stock. Bring to a boil, reduce heat and simmer until vegetables are tender while stirring often, about 15 minutes. Puree the soup in a blender until smooth, return to the pot.

2. Add the florets and gently simmer over medium heat until tender, about 5 minutes. Add the cream. Slowly add the cheese, stirring constantly. Season with salt and white pepper.

Cheesy Potato Soup with Bacon

Ingredients

Bacon, chopped	8 pieces
Onion, diced	1 each
Potatoes, peeled and diced	2 each
Flour	½ cup
Water	1¾ cup
Chicken Broth	1½ cup
Dry White Wine	¼ cup
Sharp Cheddar, grated	2 cups
Chives, chopped	2 tablespoons

Preparation

1. Cook the bacon in a heavy stock pot over medium high heat, stirring occasionally until it begins to brown. Remove the bacon with a slotted spoon and drain on paper towels.

2. Add the onion to the fat in the pot and cook until softened, about three minutes. Add potatoes, stir to mix. Add the flour and mix well. Pour in the water and chicken broth. Bring to a simmer.

3. Cook mixture until the potatoes are tender, about ten minutes. Add the wine and cook for another couple of minutes. Remove from heat and slowly stir in the cheese and chives. Taste for seasoning and serve.

Clam Chowder

Try substituting the clams with chopped smoked salmon for a rich Salmon Chowder

Ingredients

Bacon, chopped	12 pieces
Onion, diced	1 each
Celery, diced	4 stalks
Potatoes, peeled and diced	2 each
Flour	¾ cup
Clam Juice	2 quarts
Chicken Stock	1 quart
Bay Leaf	1 each
Salt	2 teaspoons
Black Pepper	1 teaspoon
Clams, chopped	2 cups
Heavy Cream	1 cup
Tabasco Sauce	½ teaspoon

Preparation

1. In a heavy bottom pot, add the bacon and cook over medium high heat stirring occasionally. Once it just begins to brown, add the celery and onions. Cook for two or three minutes.

2. Add the potatoes and flour. Stir well to mix in the flour. Add the clam juice, chicken stock, bay leaf, salt and black pepper. Bring to a simmer and cook until the potatoes are tender, about fifteen minutes.

3. Add the clams, heavy cream and Tabasco, simmer for five more minutes. Taste for seasoning and adjust as needed, serve with Seasoned Oyster Crackers (page 175).

Coconut Fish Stew

Ingredients

Olive Oil	2 tablespoons
Onion, diced	1 each
Red Bell Pepper, diced	1 each
Green Bell Pepper, diced	1 each
Yellow Bell Pepper, diced	1 each
Roma Tomatoes, seeded and diced	4 each
Jalapeno, seeded and chopped	1 each
Salt	1 teaspoon
Black Pepper	½ teaspoon
Clam Juice	3 cups
Coconut Milk	1 can (14.5 oz.)
Green Onion, whites only, chopped	8 each
Salmon, skinless, ½ " dice	1 pound
Halibut, ½ " dice	1 pound
Shrimp, peeled and chopped	1 pound
Limes, juiced	5 each
Cilantro Leaves, chopped	½ cup

Preparation

1. Heat a large pot over medium high heat and add the oil. Once it begins to smoke add the onion and peppers, cook for about five minutes or until soft. Add tomatoes, jalapeno, salt and pepper and cook for two minutes.

2. Add the clam stock and coconut milk and bring the mixture to a simmer. Adjust the heat to medium and cook for about ten minutes or until the peppers are tender. Add the green onions and all of the seafood, cover and cook for five more minutes. Stir a few times very gently while cooking.

3. Add the lime juice and cilantro and cook uncovered for five minutes. Adjust seasoning as needed and test a piece of fish. It is ready if it just breaks under gentle pressure.

Corn Chowder

Ingredients

Bacon, chopped	12 pieces
Onion, diced	1 each
Celery, diced	4 stalks
Potatoes, peeled and diced	2 each
Flour	¾ cup
Chicken Stock	3 quarts
Corn Kernels, fresh or frozen	2 cups
Thyme	2 teaspoons
Bay Leaf	1 each
Salt	2 teaspoons
Black Pepper	1 teaspoon
Heavy Cream	1 cup
Tabasco Sauce	½ teaspoon
Green Onion, thinly sliced	2 tablespoons

Preparation

1. In a heavy bottom pot, add the bacon and cook over medium high heat stirring occasionally. Once it just begins to brown, add the celery and onions. Cook for two or three minutes.

2. Add the potatoes and flour. Stir well to mix in the flour. Add half of the corn and half of the chicken stock. In a blender, puree the remaining corn and chicken stock together until very smooth and add to the pot.

3. Season with the thyme, bay leaf, salt and pepper. Bring to a simmer and cook until the potatoes are very tender, about fifteen minutes. Add the heavy cream, tabasco and green onions. Taste for seasoning and serve with Seasoned Oyster Crackers, page 175.

Cream of Mushroom Soup

Ingredients

Butter	¼ cup
Onion, diced	2 each
White Mushrooms, sliced	2 pounds
Garlic, chopped	2 cloves
White Rice, long-grain	½ cup
Chicken Stock	3½ cups
Beef Stock	3½ cups
Salt	2 teaspoons
White Pepper	1 teaspoon
Heavy Cream	½ cup
Chives, chopped	¼ cup

Preparation

1. Melt the butter in a heavy stock pot over medium high heat. Add the onions and cook until they begin to soften, about five minutes. Add the mushroom and cook, stirring often, until almost all of the liquid has evaporated, about twenty minutes.

2. Add the garlic and rice, stir well, then add the chicken stock, beef stock, salt and white pepper. Bring to a boil, reduce heat and simmer until the rice is very tender, about thirty minutes.

3. Puree the soup in a blender and return to the pot. Add the heavy cream and heat just until simmering. Remove from heat, stir in the chives and adjust seasoning as needed. More or less stock can be used to adjust the thickness of this soup.

Mexican Style Chicken Stew

Ingredients

Dried Chilies, Guajillo or Pasilla	4 each
Water, boiling hot	1 cup
Vegetable Oil	¼ cup
Corn Tortilla, cut in 1/2 " dice	5 each
Onion, diced	1 each
Green Pepper, diced	1 each
Red Pepper, diced	1 each
Corn Kernels, fresh or frozen	1 cup
Jalapeno, seeded and diced	1 each
Garlic, chopped	4 cloves
Chicken Breast, diced	1 pound
Tequila	2 ounces
Chicken Stock	3 quarts
Limes, juiced	2 each
Cilantro, chopped	1 bunch

Preparation

1. Remove the stems and seeds from the chilies and place in a bowl. Pour the boiling water on top of them and cover tightly with plastic wrap.

2. Heat the oil in a large pot over medium high heat. Once smoking, add the tortilla and fry until golden brown. Remove with a slotted spoon and drain on paper towels.

3. Add the onion, peppers, corn, jalapeno, and garlic to the pot and sauté until the vegetables are tender, about five minutes.

4. Drain the chilies, reserving some of the liquid. Puree the fried tortillas and chilies in a blender until very smooth. Add some of the chili liquid as needed to get the mixture to blend smoothly.

5. Add the chili mixture and chicken to the pot of vegetables. Cook for two minutes, stirring often. Stir in the tequila and cook for one minute. Pour in the chicken stock and bring to a boil. Reduce heat and simmer for twenty minutes or until the chicken is very tender.

6. Remove from heat and stir in the lime juice and cilantro. Season with salt and pepper as needed.

Pozole
Red Chili Pork Stew

This is a traditional Mexican Pork Stew made using dried red chilies.

Ingredients

Garlic	1 head
Country-Style Pork Ribs	4 pounds
Water, cold	12 cups
Chicken Broth	4 cups
Oregano, dried	1 teaspoon
Guajillo Chiles, dried	6 each
Water, boiled	1 ½ cups
Onion, chopped	1 each
Salt	1 tablespoon
White Hominy, drained and rinsed	4 (15 oz) cans
Lime, cut in wedges	2 each
Tortilla Chips, coarsely crushed	1 cup

Preparation

1. Peel garlic and reserve two whole cloves. Chop the rest of the garlic and add to a large heavy pot with the garlic, pork, water, and broth. Bring to a boil over medium high heat, skimming any froth that may rise to the surface. Add oregano and reduce heat to medium low. Simmer until the pork is very tender and skim the froth often. About one and a half hours.

2. While soup is simmering, discard stems and seeds from the chilies and place into a bowl. Pour the boiling hot water on top of the chilies and cover. Let sit for thirty minutes, turning the chilies occasionally. Puree the chilies with soaking water, onion, 2 teaspoons of salt, and reserved garlic in a blender until very smooth.

3. Transfer the pork to a platter and shred the meat using two forks. Discard the bones and return the meat back to the pot. Add the chili puree, hominy and remaining salt to the pot and bring to a simmer over medium high heat.

4. Reduce heat and simmer uncovered for thirty minutes, skimming the froth occasionally. Serve with lime wedges and crushed tortilla chips.

Split Pea Soup

Ingredients

Butter	3 tablespoons
Onion, chopped	2 each
Celery, chopped	1 cup
Carrots, chopped and peeled	1 cup
Smoked Pork Hocks	1 ½ pounds
Marjoram, dried	2 teaspoons
Split Peas, dried	1 ½ cup
Water	8 cups

Preparation

1. Melt the butter in a large pot over medium high heat. Add onion, celery and carrots. Cook until the vegetables begin to soften, about five minutes. Add pork and marjoram, stir for one minute. Add the peas and water and bring to a boil.

2. Reduce heat to medium low and partially cover the pot. Simmer until the pork is very tender, about one hour or a little longer. Remove the hocks and set aside. Puree half of the soup in a blender and return to the pot.

3. Cut the pork off of the bone and dice the meat. Add to the soup and season with salt and white pepper.

Southwest Chipotle Chicken Soup

Ingredients

Vegetable Oil	1 cup
Onion, diced	3 each
Potatoes, peeled and diced	2 each
Garlic, chopped	6 cloves
Jalapeno, seeded and minced	2 each
Flour	¾ cup
Chicken Stock	6 cups
Heavy Cream	4 cups
Roma Tomatoes, diced	6 each
Corn Kernels, fresh or frozen	4 cups
Monterey Jack Cheese, grated	2 cups
Parsley, chopped	2 tablespoons
Green Onion, chopped	2 tablespoons
Chicken Breast, diced	4 each
Canned Chipotle, chopped	1 each

Preparation

1. In a heavy bottom pot, add the oil and heat over medium high heat until it just begins to smoke. Add the onion, potato, garlic, and jalapeno. Cook for about five minutes, stirring occasionally.

2. Add the flour and cook for two minutes, stirring constantly. Pour in the chicken stock and bring to a simmer. Add the rest of the ingredients and return to a simmer.

3. Reduce heat and gently simmer until the potatoes are tender and the chicken is cooked, about twenty minutes. Taste and adjust seasoning with salt and pepper as needed.

Tomato Soup

Serve this with grilled cheese sandwiches for an All American meal!

Ingredients

Butter	¼ cup
Onion	2 each
Garlic, chopped	4 cloves
Tomato Paste	¼ cup
Canned Tomatoes	64 ounces
Chicken Stock	2 quarts
Basil, dried	2 teaspoons
Sugar	1 tablespoon
Salt	1 teaspoon
White Pepper	½ teaspoon
Heavy Cream	1 cup

Preparation

1. Melt the butter in a large pot over medium high heat. Add the onion and cook until very tender, stirring often, about ten minutes. Add the garlic and tomato paste and stir constantly for two minutes.

2. Add the tomatoes, chicken stock, basil, sugar, salt and white pepper. Bring to a simmer and reduce heat to medium low. Simmer, stirring occasionally, for thirty minutes. Puree the soup in a blender until very smooth.

3. Pour the pureed soup back into the pot and add the heavy cream. Heat over medium heat until just simmering. Season with salt and pepper.

Alaskan Cioppino

Serve this soup with grilled or toasted baguette bread for dipping into the broth.

Ingredients

Garlic, minced	4 cloves
White Onion, finely chopped	2 each
Bay Leaf	1 each
Dried Oregano, crumbled	1 teaspoon
Dried Red Pepper Flakes	¼ teaspoon
Salt	2 teaspoons
Black Pepper, ground	½ teaspoon
Olive Oil	¼ cup
Red Bell Pepper, diced	2 each
Tomato Paste	3 tablespoons
Red Wine, dry	1 ½ cups
Canned Tomatoes, drained, reserving juice, and chopped	1 each (32 ounces)
Clam Juice, bottled	1 cup
Chicken Broth	1 cup
King Crab	1 pound
Littleneck Clams, scrubbed	18 each
Halibut, skinless and cut into 1" cubes	1 pound
Salmon, skinless and cut into 1" cubes	1 pound
Large Shrimp, shelled and deveined	1 pound
Sea Scallops, cleaned	1 pound
Parsley, chopped	½ cup
Basil, chopped	¼ cup

Preparation

1. Heat the olive oil in a heavy pot over medium high heat and cook the garlic, onions, bay leaf, oregano, and red pepper flakes with salt and pepper until the onions begin to soften, about 5 minutes.

2. Stir in the bell pepper and tomato paste, cook while constantly stirring for 1 minute. Add the wine and bring to a boil, continue simmering until it is reduced by about half, 5 to 6 minutes.

3. Add the tomatoes and their juice, clam juice, and chicken broth. Cover and simmer for 30 minutes. Season with salt and pepper.

4. While stew is simmering, hack crab leg through shell into 2- to 3-inch pieces with a large heavy knife. Add crab pieces and clams to stew and simmer, covered, until clams just open, 5 to 10 minutes.

5. Lightly season the fish, shrimp, and scallops with salt and add to the stew. Simmer while covered just until the fish is fully cooked, about 5 minutes. Return the clams to the pot and gently stir in the parsley and basil.

6. Serve immediately in large soup bowls.

SALADS

The key to making a great salad is simple, use only the freshest ingredients possible. It is also important that they are not cluttered with unnecessary ingredients nor smothered in dressing, remember that it is only to compliment the salad and not to define it. Since they are basically raw and only require minimal preparation there is very little that can be done to improve the taste or quality of the ingredients and therefore it is absolutely necessary that the vegetables and other items are in season and are the best that you can find.

Beet and Goat Cheese Salad
with Roasted Garlic Vinaigrette

Salad Ingredients

Spring Mix Lettuce	6 cups
Beets, small	2 each
Hazelnuts, toasted and chopped	½ cup
Goat Cheese, crumbled	2 ounces
Roasted Garlic Vinaigrette	as needed

Preparation

1. Place the beets in a pot and fill with cold water to about 2 inches above the beets. Cover and bring to a boil, reduce heat and simmer until fork tender, about 1 hour. Drain and scrape off the peel using a small knife. Cut into ½" cubes and toss with a little bit of the dressing. Cover and refrigerate until needed later.

2. Rinse the lettuce under cold water and drain on paper towels inside of a pan. Cover and refrigerate.

3. Gently toss all ingredients in a large bowl immediately before serving, season with salt and pepper as needed.

Roasted Garlic Vinaigrette

Ingredients

Garlic, peeled	20 cloves
Olive Oil	2 tablespoons
Salt	1 teaspoon
Lemons, juiced	½ cup
Yellow Mustard	1 teaspoon
Sugar	1 teaspoon
Salt	1 teaspoon
White Pepper	½ teaspoon
Olive Oil, extra-virgin	1 cup
Parsley, chopped	1 tablespoon

Preparation

1. Preheat oven to 400°. In a bowl mix together the garlic, olive oil and salt. Pour into a small pan, wrap tightly with foil and bake until golden and very tender, about 45 minutes.

2. Pour the garlic and juices into a blender and add the lemon juice, mustard, sugar, salt, white pepper. Puree until smooth. With the motor running on medium high, slowly pour in the olive oil. Add the parsley and just pulse a few times to mix everything.

3. Cover and refrigerate.

Bacon, Lettuce, Tomato and Turkey Salad with French Dressing

Salad Ingredients

Romaine Lettuce	½ head
Iceberg Lettuce	½ head
Bacon, chopped	¼ pound
Tomatoes	2 each
Turkey, cooked	¼ pound
Croutons, plain or seasoned	1 cup
French Dressing	as needed

Preparation

1. Begin by chopping both types of lettuce and rinsing under cold water. Drain on paper towels inside of a pan. Cover and refrigerate.

2. Cook the bacon in a heavy pan over medium high heat stirring often, until golden brown. Drain and place on paper towels, set aside.

3. Remove the core from the tomatoes and cut into thin wedges about ¼" thick. Cut the turkey into ½" cubes or slices as you prefer.

4. Gently toss all ingredients in a large bowl immediately before serving, season with salt and pepper as needed.

French Dressing

Ingredients

Rice Wine Vinegar	⅓ cup
Sugar	⅓ cup
Ketchup	½ cup
Garlic, chopped	1 clove
Onion, minced	¼ cup
Salt	1 teaspoon
White Pepper	¼ teaspoon
Olive Oil, extra-virgin	½ cup

Preparation

1. Using a blender add the vinegar, sugar, ketchup, garlic, onion, salt and white pepper. Mix on high until smooth.

2. With the motor running on medium high, slowly pour in the oil. Cover and refrigerate.

Tomato and Cucumber Salad with Blue Cheese Dressing

Salad Ingredients

Romaine Lettuce	1 head
Iceberg Lettuce	1 head
Radicchio	2 heads
Tomato	3 each
Cucumber	1 each
Red Onion, small	1 each
Croutons, seasoned or plain	1 cup
Blue Cheese Dressing	½-1 cup
Salt and Black Pepper	as needed

Preparation

1. Chop the lettuces and rinse under cold water. Drain on paper towels inside of a pan. Cover and refrigerate. Remove the core from the tomatoes and cut into thin wedges about ¼" thick. Trim the ends off the cucumber and cut into thin slices about 2" long. Peel the onion, cut off the root end and slice very thin.

2. Gently toss all ingredients in a large bowl shortly before serving. Use as much dressing as you prefer and season with salt and pepper.

Blue Cheese Dressing

Ingredients

Mayonnaise	¼ cup
Sour Cream	¼ cup
Buttermilk	1 tablespoon
Blue Cheese, crumbled	1 cup
Lemon, juiced	1 tablespoon
Parsley, chopped	1 tablespoon
Salt	¼ teaspoon
Black Pepper	¼ teaspoon

Preparation

1. In a large bowl whisk together the mayonnaise, sour cream, and buttermilk. Be sure to break up any lumps of mayonnaise that may remain.

2. Add the remaining ingredients, mix well, cover and refrigerate for at least an hour before using.

Caesar Salad

Salad Ingredients

Romaine Lettuce	3 heads
Celery	2 stalks
Sundried Tomatoes	¾ cup
Parsley, washed	1 bunch
Capers, drained and rinsed	¼ cup
Parmesan Cheese, grated	1 cup
Croutons, seasoned or plain	1 cup
Caesar Dressing	½-1 cup
Salt and Black Pepper	as needed

Preparation

1. Chop the lettuce and rinse under cold water. Drain on paper towels inside of a pan. Cover and refrigerate. Cut the celery into very thin slices about 1½" long. Cut the tomatoes into slices ¼" thick. Pick just the small leaves from the parsley, tearing any large ones in half.

2. Gently toss all ingredients in a large bowl shortly before serving. Use as much dressing as you prefer and season with salt and pepper.

Caesar Dressing

Ingredients

Garlic, minced	2 cloves
Salt	¼ teaspoon
Anchovy Paste	1 teaspoon
Lemon Juice	2 tablespoon
Dijon Mustard	1 teaspoon
Whole Grain Mustard	1 teaspoon
Worcestershire Sauce	1 teaspoon
Mayonnaise	1 cup
Parmesan Cheese, grated	½ cup
Black Pepper	1 teaspoon

Preparation

1. Smash the garlic and salt against a cutting board using the side of a knife blade until it is a coarse paste.

2. Add the garlic paste, anchovy, lemon juice, dijon mustard, whole grain mustard and worcestershire sauce to a bowl and mix using a whisk. Add the mayonnaise, parmesan cheese and black pepper. Mix well to break up any lumps of mayonnaise.

3. Cover and refrigerate.

Chef Salad
with House Dressing

Salad Ingredients

Romaine Lettuce	1 head
Iceberg Lettuce	1 head
Radicchio Lettuce	1 head
Eggs, hard boiled	6 each
Turkey, deli sliced	4 ounces
Ham, deli sliced	4 ounces
Roast Beef, deli sliced	4 ounces
Cheddar Cheese, grated	1 cup
Tomato	2 each
Red Onion, small	1 each
Croutons, seasoned or plain	1 cup
House Dressing	1 – 2 cups
Salt and Black Pepper	as needed

Preparation

1. Chop the lettuce and rinse under cold water. Drain on paper towels inside of a pan. Cover and refrigerate. Peel and then slice or chop the eggs. Slice all of the deli meats into ¼" strips. Remove the core from the tomatoes and cut into thin wedges about ¼" thick. Peel the onion, cut off the root end and slice very thin.

2. Gently toss all ingredients in a large bowl shortly before serving, and gently mix in the dressings using half Ranch and half French. Use as much dressing as you prefer and season with salt and pepper.

House Dressing

Ingredients

Mayonnaise	¾ cup
Buttermilk	½ cup
Ketchup	½ cup
Olive Oil, extra-virgin	½ cup
Sugar	⅓ cup
Red Wine Vinegar	¼ cup
Onion, minced	3 tablespoons
Parsley, chopped	2 tablespoons
Lemon, juiced	2 tablespoons
Dijon Mustard	2 teaspoons
Garlic Powder	1 teaspoon
Salt	1 tablespoon
Black Pepper	2 teaspoons

Preparation

1. In a large bowl, gently beat together all ingredients with a whisk until smooth and well mixed. Cover and refrigerate until needed.

Ham and Swiss Salad
With Thousand Island Dressing

Salad Ingredients

Romaine Lettuce	1 head
Iceberg Lettuce	1 head
Ham, deli sliced	4 ounces
Swiss Cheese, grated	1 cup
Croutons, seasoned or plain	1 cup
Thousand Island Dressing	½-1 cup
Salt and Black Pepper	as needed

Preparation

1. Chop the lettuces and rinse under cold water. Drain on paper towels inside of a pan. Cover and refrigerate. Slice the ham into ¼" strips

2. Gently toss all ingredients in a large bowl shortly before serving. Use as much dressing as you prefer and season with salt and pepper.

Thousand Island Dressing

Ingredients

Mayonnaise	¾ cup
Chili Sauce	¼ cup
Ketchup	2 tablespoons
Onion, minced	2 tablespoons
Sweet Pickle Relish, drained	1 tablespoon
Garlic, minced	1 clove
Hard-Boiled Egg, chopped	1 each
Salt	½ teaspoon
White Pepper	¼ teaspoon

Preparation

1. In a mixing bowl whisk together the mayonnaise, chili sauce, and ketchup. Add the rest of the ingredients and mix well.

2. Cover and refrigerate.

Bacon, Egg, and Cheese Salad
With Ranch Dressing

Salad Ingredients

Romaine Lettuce	3 heads
Bacon	½ pound
Eggs	6 each
Cheddar Cheese, grated	1 cup
Croutons, plain or seasoned	1 cup
Ranch Dressing	½ - 1 cup
Salt and Black Pepper	to taste

Preparation

1. Cut the bacon into thin strips and put into a pan over medium high heat. Cook, stirring occasionally, until crispy and golden brown. About 7 – 10 minutes. Drain on paper towels.

2. Place the eggs into a small pot and add enough water to cover them by 1". Bring to a boil, uncovered, over high heat. Once at a full rolling boil, cover and remove from heat. Set a twelve minute timer, once done remove eggs and put into a bowl of ice water. Set aside until cooled and then peel and slice the eggs. Cover and refrigerate.

3. Chop the lettuce and rinse under cold water. Drain on paper towels inside of a pan. Cover and refrigerate.

4. Gently toss all ingredients in a large bowl shortly before serving. Use as much dressing as you prefer and season with salt and pepper.

Ranch Dressing

Ingredients

Mayonnaise	¾ cup
Buttermilk	½ cup
Dry Milk, or Powdered Buttermilk	2 tablespoons
Parsley, chopped	2 tablespoons
Onion, minced	1 tablespoon
Lemon, juiced	2 tablespoons
Dijon Mustard	2 teaspoons
Garlic Powder	½ teaspoon
Salt	1 tablespoon
Black Pepper	2 teaspoons

Preparation

1. In a large bowl whisk together the mayonnaise, buttermilk and milk powder. Be sure to break up any lumps of mayonnaise that may remain.

2. Add the remaining ingredients, mix well, cover and refrigerate for at least an hour before using.

Reuben Salad
With Russian Dressing

Salad Ingredients

Romaine Lettuce	3 heads
Pastrami, deli sliced	½ pound
Sauerkraut, drained	½ cup
Swiss Cheese, grated	1 cup
Croutons, preferably Rye	1 cup
Russian Dressing	½ - 1 cup
Salt and Black Pepper	to taste

Preparation

1. Chop the lettuce and rinse under cold water. Drain on paper towels inside of a pan. Cover and refrigerate. Cut the pastrami into small pieces

2. Gently toss all ingredients in a large bowl shortly before serving. Use as much dressing as you prefer and season with salt and pepper.

Russian Dressing

Ingredients

Mayonnaise	⅔ cup
Ketchup	⅓ cup
Dill Pickle Relish	¼ cup
Onion, minced	¼ cup
Salt	2 teaspoons
White Pepper	1 teaspoon
Paprika	½ teaspoon

Preparation

1. In a mixing bowl, whisk together all of the ingredients until smooth.

2. Cover and refrigerate.

Salami and Mozzarella Salad with Italian Dressing

Salad Ingredients

Radicchio Lettuce	2 heads
Romaine Lettuce	1 head
Tomatoes	2 each
Red Onion, small	1 each
Salami, ½" cubes	1 cup
Mozzarella Cheese, ½" cubes	¾ cup
Green Olives, sliced	½ cup
Croutons, plain or seasoned	1 cup
Italian Dressing	as needed

Preparation

1. Begin by chopping both types of lettuce and rinsing under cold water. Drain on paper towels inside of a pan. Cover and refrigerate.

2. Remove the core from the tomatoes and cut into thin wedges about ¼" thick. Peel the onion, cut off the root end and slice very thin.

3. Gently toss all ingredients in a large bowl immediately before serving, season with salt and pepper as needed.

Italian Dressing

Ingredients

Apple Cider Vinegar	3 tablespoons
Garlic Clove, chopped	2 each
Sugar	½ teaspoon
Salt	½ teaspoon
Black Pepper	¼ teaspoon
Olive Oil, extra-virgin	½ cup
Red Pepper Flakes	⅛ teaspoon
Parmesan Cheese, grated	2 tablespoons

Preparation

1. Using a blender add the vinegar, garlic, sugar, salt and black pepper. Mix on high until smooth.

2. With the motor running on medium high, slowly pour in the oil. Add the red pepper flakes and parmesan cheese and just pulse a few times to mix everything together. Cover and refrigerate.

Simple Garden Salad
with Sweet Balsamic Dressing

Salad Ingredients

Romaine Lettuce	1 head
Carrot, peeled	1 each
Cucumber	½ each
Tomatoes	2 each
Red Onion, small	1 each
Croutons, plain or seasoned	1 cup
Sweet Balsamic Dressing	as needed

Preparation

1. Begin by chopping both types of lettuce and rinsing under cold water. Drain on paper towels inside of a pan. Cover and refrigerate.

2. Trim the ends off of the carrot, cut in half lengthwise and then into very thin slices about 1½" long. Repeat with the cucumber.

3. Remove the core from the tomatoes and cut into thin wedges about ¼" thick. Peel the onion, cut off the root end and slice very thin.

4. Gently toss all ingredients in a large bowl immediately before serving, season with salt and pepper as needed.

Sweet Balsamic Dressing

Ingredients

Balsamic Vinegar, good quality	½ cup
Honey	2 tablespoons
Olive Oil, extra virgin	½ cup
Green Onion, white part only, chopped	1 tablespoon
Garlic, chopped	2 teaspoon
Salt	1 teaspoon
Black Pepper	½ teaspoon

Preparation

1. Using a blender puree together the vinegar and honey. With the motor running on medium high, slowly drizzle in the oil.

2. Add the green onion, garlic, salt and pepper and pulse a few times to mix well. Cover and refrigerate.

HALIBUT

Halibut is my favorite fish to work with because it has a neutral flavor and wonderful texture that lends itself nicely to any style of cuisine from Latin to Italian or Asian, it is just so good. Like any fresh fish it should not be complicated or burdened with unnecessary ingredients and intricate preparations. The real trick to cooking Halibut, to compliment the fish and make it shine, is to keep it fresh and simple and do not let it get overcooked!

Halibut Cooking Tip

When preparing Halibut it can quickly become overcooked so it is important to know when to remove it from the heat. As a rule I usually stop cooking it once it is a little more than half way cooked, remove it from the heat (grill, oven, etc.) and loosely cover it with foil and allow it to rest in a warm area while I finish getting everything else ready. So using a small sharp knife, gently poke the center and look into the piece of fish, when only the center third is still translucent the Halibut is done. It will continue to cook and in ten minutes or so it will be fully cooked but not dry or tough. When Halibut is overcooked it is almost inedible, and this is the most common problem people have when first learning how to cook Halibut.

Bacon Wrapped Halibut with Red Pepper Sauce

Ingredients

Halibut Filet, skinless and boneless	3 pounds
Bacon, thick slices	1 – 2 pounds, as needed
Red Peppers	3 each
Olive Oil	2 tablespoons
Heavy Cream	2 cups
Rosemary, 3" piece	1 sprig
Lemon, juiced	1 each
Sugar	2 teaspoons
Salt and White Pepper	as needed

Preparation

1. Toss the peppers in a bowl with 1 tablespoon of olive oil and a little bit of salt. Over a gas burner or on a hot grill roast the peppers until charred all over on all sides. Remove and place in a bowl then cover tightly with plastic wrap. Once cooled, remove the seeds and peel the skin off of the peppers.

2. In a sauce pot over medium high heat add the roasted peppers, heavy cream, and rosemary. Simmer until reduced by about one third. Remove from heat season with salt and pepper and take out the rosemary. Once cooled slightly puree in a blender or food processor until very smooth. Return to the pot, cover, and keep warm.

3. Cut the halibut into long rectangular pieces about 2" wide and 2" thick. Season with salt and pepper. Lay the bacon on a work surface so that the edges of each slice overlap just a little, using enough slices to extend the length of the halibut pieces. Place the fish on one side of the loose ends of the bacon and carefully roll to wrap tightly with the bacon. Trim off the bacon when necessary so as not to use more than what is needed to create one wrap around the fish that overlaps by about 1" on the underside.

4. Heat a skillet over medium high heat and add 1 tablespoon of olive oil. When hot but not smoking, place the wrapped fish pieces in and cook until golden on all sides, about 2 minutes per side. Remove and place onto a baking pan with a rack inside. Cook in the oven until firm and the center is fully cooked, test by cutting into one piece. Remove and let rest for a few minutes.

5. Slice the fish into 1½" slices and arrange neatly on a platter, drizzle with the sauce and serve.

Baked Halibut with Swiss and Mushrooms

Ingredients

Halibut, skinless	2 pounds
Mayonnaise	½ cup
Sour Cream	½ cup
Lemon, juiced	1 each
Onion, minced	½ each
Tabasco Sauce	1 teaspoon
Mushrooms, sliced	2 cups
Olive Oil	¼ cup
Swiss Cheese, grated	2 cups
Green Onion, sliced	2 tablespoons
Salt and White Pepper	as needed

Preparation

1. Preheat the oven to 375°.

2. In a small bowl stir together the mayonnaise, sour cream, lemon juice, onion and Tabasco sauce.

3. Heat the olive oil is a large skillet over high heat. Once smoking add the mushrooms and cook until softened and most of the liquid is absorbed, about 5 minutes. Season with salt and pepper and drain.

4. Cut the halibut into 6 equal pieces, season with salt and white pepper. Place into a baking dish and spread the mayonnaise mixture on each piece. Top with the sautéed mushrooms and sprinkle with the cheese. Bake until the center is opaque and the fish breaks easily when tested with a fork, about 12 minutes. Remove from the oven.

5. Preheat the broiler.

6. Return the fish to the oven and boil until the cheese is golden brown and bubbling, about 3 minutes. Transfer fish to a platter and sprinkle with the green onion.

Beer Battered Halibut

Ingredients

Halibut, skinless and boneless	2 pounds
Flour	1 cup
Beer, cold	1 cup
Salt	1 teaspoon
Paprika	¼ teaspoon
Vegetable Oil	4 – 6 cups

Preparation

1. Cut the halibut into even sized pieces about 1" wide, 3 "long, and ½" thick. Refrigerate.

2. Whisk together the flour and beer in a bowl, gently mixing just enough until smooth. Stir in the salt and paprika.

3. Pour the oil into a deep pot to a depth of 2" and heat over medium high to 375°.

4. Coat a piece of fish with the batter and allow any excess to drain off and then carefully lower into the oil. Fry, turning once, until golden brown. Remove with tongs and drain on paper towels. Repeat with the remaining fish.

5. Serve with Tartar Sauce (page 174) or Lemon Aioli (page 170).

Broiled Halibut with Lemon and Caramelized Onion

Ingredients

Halibut, skinless and boneless	3 pounds
Olive Oil	2 tablespoons
Butter, cold, ¼" cubes	¼ cup
Lemon, juiced	2 each
Butter	¼ cup
Onion, thin slices	2 each
Garlic, chopped	2 tablespoons
Thyme, chopped	1 tablespoon
Sugar	1 tablespoon
Salt and White Pepper	as needed

Preparation

1. In a heavy pot melt the butter over medium high heat. Add the onions and season with salt and pepper. Cook until the onions are tender but do not have any color, about 5 minutes. Reduce heat to medium or medium low, add the garlic, thyme and sugar. Continue cooking until very tender and golden, about 30 minutes.

2. Cut the halibut into six even sized pieces. Season generously with salt and pepper. Heat the olive oil in a large skillet over medium high heat. Once smoking place three pieces of fish, skin side up, in the pan and cook until very golden, about 4 minutes. Remove and place on a foil lined baking pan. Repeat with remaining fish pieces.

3. Preheat the broiler.

4. Squeeze the lemon juice on top of the fish and place a few cubes of butter onto each piece. Broil until the center is opaque and it easily breaks when tested with a fork, about 4 minutes.

5. Spread the onions onto a platter and nestle the fish in the onions. Serve immediately.

Buffalo Halibut

Ingredients

Halibut, skinless and boneless	2 pounds
Flour	1 cup
Garlic Powder	1 teaspoon
Celery Salt	1 teaspoon
Vegetable Oil	4 – 6 cups
Hot Sauce, Frank's	½ cup
Butter, melted	¼ cup
Blue Cheese, crumbled	1 cup

Preparation

1. Cut the halibut into small 1" pieces. Refrigerate. Whisk together the flour, garlic powder and celery salt in a large bowl.

2. Pour the oil into a deep pot to a depth of 2" and heat over medium high to 375°. Using a blender or electric mixer, stir together the hot sauce and butter, set aside.

3. Toss several pieces of fish in the flour and gently coat. Lift with a slotted spoon and shake to remove any excess flour before carefully lowering into the oil. Fry, stirring occasionally, until golden brown. Remove with a slotted metal spoon and drain on paper towels. Repeat with the remaining fish.

4. Place the fish on a platter and drizzle with the hot sauce and then sprinkle with the crumbled blue cheese. Serve immediately.

Coconut Fried Halibut

Ingredients

Halibut, skinless and boneless	2 pounds
Flour	1 cup
Beer, cold	1 cup
Coconut, grated	1 cup
Salt	1 teaspoon
Vegetable Oil	4 – 6 cups

Preparation

1. Cut the halibut into even sized pieces about 1" wide, 3 "long, and ½" thick. Refrigerate.

2. Whisk together the flour and beer in a bowl, gently mixing just enough until smooth. Stir in the coconut and salt.

3. Pour the oil into a deep pot to a depth of 2" and heat over medium high to 375°.

4. Coat a piece of fish with the batter and allow any excess to drain off and then carefully lower into the oil. Fry, turning once, until golden brown. Remove with tongs and drain on paper towels. Repeat with the remaining fish.

5. Serve with Tartar Sauce (page 174) or Chili Aioli (page 171).

Chef TJ Weston

Drunken Halibut with Sherry Cream Sauce

Ingredients

Halibut, skinless and boneless	3 pounds
Olive Oil	2 tablespoons
White Onion, minced	¼ cup
Sherry	½ cup
Heavy Cream	2 cups
Tomatoes, seeded and chopped	2 each
Capers, rinsed	¼ cup
Parsley, chopped	2 tablespoons
Lemon, juiced	1 each
Salt and White Pepper	as needed

Preparation

1. Cut the halibut into six even sized pieces. Season generously with salt and pepper. Heat the olive oil in a large skillet over medium high heat. Once smoking place three pieces of fish, skin side up, in the pan and cook until very golden, about 4 minutes. Remove and set on a plate loosely covered with foil. Repeat with remaining fish pieces.

2. Add the onion to the pan and cook until tender, carefully add the sherry and simmer until almost dry. Return the fish, seared side up, to the pan along with the cream, tomatoes, capers, parsley and lemon juice.

3. Simmer until the sauce is slightly reduced and thickened, about 5 minutes. Season with salt and pepper. Test a piece of fish by gently pressing and if it breaks easily and the center is slightly opaque it is done.

4. Put the fish onto a platter and spoon the sauce on top of each piece. Serve immediately.

Grilled Halibut with Citrus Butter

Ingredients

Halibut, skinless and boneless	3 pounds
Olive Oil	2 tablespoons
Oranges, juiced	2 each
White Wine	½ cup
Garlic, chopped	1 tablespoon
Butter, softened	½ cup
Lemon, zested and juiced	1 each
Lime, zested and juiced	1 each
Cilantro, chopped	¼ cup
Salt and White Pepper	as needed

Preparation

1. In a bowl stir together the olive oil, orange juice, white wine and garlic. Cut the halibut into six even sized pieces. Place into the orange juice marinade and refrigerate for 1 – 4 hours. Drain and season generously with salt and pepper.

2. Using an electric mixer whip the butter until light and fluffy. Gently stir in the lemon zest and juice, the lime zest and juice and the cilantro. Season with salt and white pepper.

3. Heat the grill to medium high heat and spray with non stick spray. Cook the halibut until just opaque in the center, about 3 minutes per side. Spread some of the butter on top of each piece of fish during the last few minutes of cooking. Remove to a serving tray and spread with a little more butter. Serve immediately.

Herb Crusted Halibut with Tomato Butter

Ingredients

Halibut, skinless	2 pounds
Panko Bread Crumbs	2 cups
Parsley, chopped	1 bunch
Butter, melted	½ cup
Tomato Sauce, seasoned	1 cup
Butter, softened	½ cup
Salt and White Pepper	as needed

Preparation

1. Using a food processor blend together the bread crumbs and parsley until very smooth and green, pour into a shallow pan. Cut the halibut into 6 equal pieces, season with salt and pepper.

2. Carefully hold a piece of halibut and dip the top surface into the butter, allow any excess to drain off, then gently press into the bread crumb mixture a few times. Place onto a rack in a baking pan and repeat with the remaining pieces.

3. Heat the tomato sauce in a small pot until simmering, pour into a blender, add the softened butter and blend on high until light in color, about 30 seconds. Season with salt and pepper. Set aside.

4. Place the breaded halibut into the oven and bake until just opaque in the center, about 8 – 10 minutes. Pour the tomato butter onto a serving platter and place the cooked fish on top. Serve immediately.

Sautéed Halibut with Capers and Tomatoes

Ingredients

Halibut, skinless and boneless	3 pounds
Olive Oil	2 tablespoons
Tomatoes, seeded and chopped	5 each
Capers, rinsed	½ cup
White Onion, minced	¼ cup
Olive Oil, extra virgin	¼ cup
Parsley, chopped	2 tablespoons
Lemon, juiced	1 each
Salt and White Pepper	as needed

Preparation

1. In a bowl stir together the tomatoes, capers, onion, extra virgin olive oil, parsley, and lemon juice. Season with salt and white pepper. Set aside.

2. Cut the halibut into six even sized pieces. Season generously with salt and pepper. Heat the olive oil in a large skillet over medium high heat. Once smoking place three pieces of fish, skin side up, in the pan and cook until very golden, about 4 minutes. Turn and continue cooking until the center is opaque, about 3 minutes. Remove and set on a plate loosely covered with foil. Repeat with remaining fish pieces.

3. Put the fish onto a platter and spoon the tomato mixture on top of each piece of fish. Serve immediately.

Seared Halibut with Caper Cream

Ingredients

Halibut, skinless and boneless	3 pounds
Olive Oil	4 tablespoons
Capers, rinsed	½ cup
White Onion, minced	¼ cup
White Wine	½ cup
Heavy Cream	2 cup
Parsley, chopped	2 tablespoons
Lemon, juiced	1 each
Salt and White Pepper	as needed

Preparation

1. Preheat oven to 425°.

2. In a sauce pot over medium high heat add two tablespoons of olive oil, capers, and white onion. Cook, stirring often, until the onion is soft and translucent, about 4 minutes. Add the white wine and increase the heat to high, simmer until almost all of the liquid is evaporated. Reduce heat to medium high, add the heavy cream and simmer until reduced by one half. Remove from heat and stir in the parsley, season with salt and pepper.

3. Cut the halibut into six even sized pieces. Season generously with salt and pepper. Heat the remaining two tablespoons of the olive oil in a large skillet over medium high heat. Once smoking place three pieces of fish, skin side up, in the pan and cook until very golden, about 4 minutes. Remove and set on a baking pan lined with foil, seared side up. Repeat with remaining fish pieces.

4. Put the fish in the oven and cook until just the center is opaque and the fish breaks easily when tested with a fork, about 8 minutes. Transfer to a serving tray and spoon the sauce on top of each piece.

Simple Grilled Halibut

Ingredients

Halibut, skinless and boneless	3 pounds
Beer	12 ounces
Soy Sauce	1 cup
Brown Sugar	1 cup
Olive Oil	2 tablespoons
Butter, melted	¼ cup
Lemon, juiced	2 each
Salt and White Pepper	as needed

Preparation

1. In a bowl stir together the beer, soy sauce and brown sugar. Cut the halibut into six even sized pieces. Place into the beer marinade and refrigerate for 1 – 4 hours. Drain and season generously with salt and pepper and then coat with the olive oil.

2. In a small bowl whisk together the melted butter and lemon juice.

3. Heat the grill to medium high heat and spray with non stick spray. Cook the halibut until just opaque in the center, about 3 minutes per side. Brush with the lemon butter during the last few minutes of cooking. Remove to a serving tray and brush with a little more butter. Serve immediately.

Sweet and Sour Halibut Stir Fry

Ingredients

Halibut, skinless, 1" pieces	2 pounds
Cornstarch	1 cup
Vegetable Oil	½ cup
Onion, ½" dice	1 each
Red Pepper, ½" dice	1 each
Broccoli, small florets	1 cup
Pineapple, ½" dice	1 cup
Mushrooms, thin slice	1 cup
Sweet and Sour Sauce, page 172	2 cups
Cilantro, chopped	½ cup
Sesame Seeds	2 tablespoons
Salt and White Pepper	as needed

Preparation

1. Heat a couple tablespoons of the oil in a large skillet until smoking. Toss some of the halibut in the cornstarch and shake off any excess, then carefully add to the oil. Cook until lightly golden, gently stirring often.

2. Add some of the vegetables, season with salt and white pepper and continue cooking and stirring until tender, about 3 minutes.

3. Pour in some of the sauce and stir to coat everything. Transfer to a platter and cover loosely with foil while repeating the process and cooking in small batches.

4. Right before serving sprinkle with the cilantro and sesame seeds.

SALMON

Wild Alaskan Salmon is some of the greatest seafood available and can make a wonderful entrée for diner, a nice accompaniment to a light salad, and is fantastic cured and smoked. It is very versatile and works best with just simple and straightforward preparations that underscore its robust flavor.

Salmon Cooking Tip

No matter the portion size or how it is being cooked, the best way to judge when the salmon is done cooking is to watch for it to begin "milking" which is when tiny white beads of protein appear on the surface. This indicates a moist translucent center that is neither too red nor dry. The fork method also works well, simply push against the center of the fish with the side of a fork. If it flakes easily under gentle pressure then it is finished. But of course you can also just break a piece open for a better look.

Almond Crusted Salmon with Red Wine Butter

Ingredients

Salmon, skin and bones removed	3 pounds
Salt and White Pepper	as needed
Fresh Ginger, grated and chopped	2 tablespoons
Almonds, sliced and untoasted	1 cup
Butter, melted	¼ cup
Beef Stock	1 cup
Rosemary, 3" piece	1 sprig
Dry Red Wine	1 cup
Sugar	2 teaspoons
Butter, cold and cut into ½" cubes	1 cup

Preparation

1. Preheat oven to 375°.

2. In a heavy sauce pot boil the beef stock and rosemary over high heat. Reduce the temperature and simmer until about ¼ cup of liquid remains. Add the wine and sugar and continue simmering until ¼ cup of liquid remains in the pot. Remove from the heat and use a wire whisk to stir in the cold butter, a few pieces at a time. Remove the rosemary and check for seasoning. Cover and keep in a warm place until needed.

3. Cut the salmon into six equal pieces and place onto a foil lined baking pan and season with salt and pepper. Top each piece with a little bit of the ginger and a layer of almonds and then drizzle with the melted butter.

4. Bake until the center of the salmon is opaque, about 7 – 10 minutes. Remove from the oven and transfer to a platter. Drizzle each piece with some of the red wine butter or serve it on the side.

Baked Salmon Cacciatore

I recommend serving this over boiled egg noodles or steamed white rice

Ingredients

Salmon Filet, skinless with bones removed	1 each, about 3 pounds
Olive Oil	2 tablespoons
Onion, chopped	1 each
Red Bell Pepper, chopped	1 each
Garlic, chopped	2 cloves
Capers, rinsed	¼ cup
Dry Red Wine	¾ cup
Diced Tomatoes	1 can, 28 ounces
Chicken Stock	¾ cup
Lemon, seeded and sliced thin	1 each
Parsley, chopped	¼ cup
Salt and White Pepper	as needed

Preparation

1. Preheat oven to 350°.

2. Cut the salmon into 6 or 8 equal sized pieces and pat dry with a paper towel. Season on all sides with a little salt and white pepper. Heat the oil in a large heavy skillet over medium high heat until hot but not smoking. Cook a few pieces of fish skin side up until golden brown, about 3 minutes. Transfer to a casserole dish or baking pan and place with the cooked side up. Repeat with the remaining fish pieces.

3. Add the onion, bell pepper, garlic, and capers to the skillet and reduce the heat to medium. Cook, stirring often, until the onions are golden, about 10 minutes. Return to medium high heat and add the wine. Cook until the liquid is reduced by half, about 5 minutes. Add the tomatoes with their juice and the chicken stock. While simmering break up the tomatoes a little with a wooden spoon and scrape up any brown bits that may stick to the pan. Cook for ten more minutes.

4. Stir in the parsley and lemon then season with salt and white pepper. Pour over the salmon and cover with foil. Bake until the salmon flakes easily, about 20 – 25 minutes.

BBQ Salmon

Ingredients

Salmon Filet	1 each, about 3 pounds
BBQ Dry Rub, page 165	½ cup
Traditional BBQ Sauce, page 166	1 cup

Preparation

1. Preheat the grill with the fire on just one side, maintaining a temperature around 325° – 350°. Add a few handfuls of wood chips and wait until it begins smoking.

2. Season the salmon with the dry rub and place on the grill, opposite the fire. Cook with the lid down until the salmon is just opaque in the center, about 25 – 30 minutes. Adjust the fire and wood chips as needed to control the temperature and amount of smoke.

3. Begin basting the salmon with the barbecue sauce a few times during the last 10 minutes of cooking. Remove from the grill and transfer to a serving platter. Serve immediately.

Broiled Salmon with Lemon-Dill Butter

Ingredients

Salmon Filet, bones removed	1 each, about 3 pounds
Salt and White Pepper	as needed
Onion, thinly sliced	1 each
Lemon, thinly sliced	1 each
Butter, softened	½ cup
Lemon, juiced	1 each
Dill, chopped	2 tablespoons

Preparation

1. Preheat broiler.

2. Place the fish onto a foil lined baking pan and season generously with salt and white pepper, top with one thin layer of the onion and lemon slices. Broil until the salmon is just opaque in the center, about 8 minutes.

3. Using an electric mixer whip the butter until light and fluffy. Add the lemon juice and chopped dill, stir to mix well.

4. Gently scrape the onion and lemon off the salmon and coat with half of the butter mixture. Continue broiling until golden on top, about 2 – 3 minutes. Remove from oven and spread the remaining butter on to the salmon, transfer to a platter and serve with the lemon and onion slices if you prefer.

Cedar Plank Salmon with Sautéed Veggies

Ingredients

Salmon filet, skinless with bones removed	1 each, about 3 pounds
Olive Oil	4 tablespoons
Salt and White Pepper	as needed
Butter	¼ cup
Zucchini, seeded and diced	2 each
Tomatoes, seeded and diced	6 each
Garlic, chopped	1 tablespoon
Basil, chopped	1 tablespoon
Salt and White Pepper	as needed

Preparation

1. Preheat oven to 500°.

2. Cut the salmon into 8 equal sized portions. Season with salt and white pepper.

3. Heat a large skillet over medium high heat. Add half of the oil and once smoking, place four pieces of fish skin side up into the pan. Cook until golden brown, rotating in the pan once, about 3 minutes. Remove and place skin side down onto a dry cedar plank. Repeat with remaining fish.

4. Melt the butter in a heavy pot over medium high heat. Add the zucchini and increase the heat to high, cook until tender, about 4 minutes. Add the tomatoes and garlic, cook for another minute. Stir in the basil and season with salt and white pepper. Remove from heat and cover.

5. Place the cedar boards into the oven on the highest rack and cook until the fish is just opaque in the center and flakes easily when tested with a fork, about 5 minutes. Remove and serve immediately with the vegetables spooned on top.

Cold Smoked Salmon

Ingredients

Salmon Filet	1 each, about 5 pounds
Salt, kosher	8 cups
Brown Sugar, packed	4 cups
Rum, dark	2 ounces

Preparation

1. Wrap the salmon in several layers of paper towel and then wrap in several sheets of newspaper. Place onto a tray and weight it down with a casserole dish or other item. Refrigerate overnight.

2. Unwrap the salmon and rinse under cold running water and then pat dry with paper towels. Find a pan large enough to hold the salmon, trimming from the tail end if necessary. Line the pan with plastic wrap.

3. Mix together the salt and sugar. Place a layer of the salt mixture in the pan about ½" thick. Set the fish on top with the skin side down and coat with the remaining mixture. Apply more on the thicker parts of the filet and a little less on the thinner parts. Refrigerate, untouched, for three full days.

4. Remove the fish from the pan and gently rinse off under cold running water. Feel the thickest part of the filet, it should feel dense and firm with just a little give to it, similar to a slab of bacon. If it seems too soft, repeat the salting process for another three days, testing the salmon each day. When it is ready, rinse under cold running water and pat dry with paper towels.

5. Use a clean cloth to wipe the rum over the entire surface of the salmon. Refrigerate overnight uncovered and preferably directly under the fan. Should feel slightly tacky in the morning.

6. Prepare the smoker to 70° with a light smoke.

7. Spray the smoker rack with non-stick spray and place the salmon in the center. Smoke the salmon for one hour and then increase the amount of smoke to high. Continue smoking for 24 – 48 hours depending on the amount of flavor you prefer. Remove the salmon and rub the surface with a little oil. Refrigerate uncovered overnight before wrapping and storing.

Crispy Fried Salmon

Ingredients

Salmon filet, skinless with bones removed	1 each, about 3 pounds
Flour	2 cups
Garlic Powder	2 teaspoons
White Pepper	1 teaspoon
Milk	2 cups
Mayonnaise	1 cup
Bread Crumbs	2 cups
Dill Weed, dried	1 tablespoon
Vegetable Oil	2 cups

Preparation

1. Cut the salmon into evenly sized pieces about 1" wide, 3" long and ½" thick. Refrigerate.

2. Mix the flour, garlic powder, and white pepper together and place into a pie plate or shallow pan. Pour the milk and mayonnaise into a second pan and mix well with a fork or whisk to break up any lumps. Put the breadcrumbs and dill weed into a third pan. Take a piece of fish and gently coat it in the flour and carefully shake off any excess, then dip into the milk mixture and drain any excess before coating with the bread crumbs. Place the breaded fish onto a tray and repeat with the remaining pieces of fish.

3. Add the vegetable oil to a pot until about 1½ inches deep. Heat over medium to medium high heat until hot but not smoking. Add a few pieces of the breaded fish and fry until golden brown, turning occasionally to ensure even cooking, remove with tongs and drain on a paper towel. Season with salt while still hot. Cover the cooked fish loosely with a piece of foil while continuing to fry the remaining pieces.

4. Serve with either Tartar Sauce (page 174) or Lemon Aioli (page 170).

Grilled Salmon with Creamy Horseradish

Ingredients

Salmon Filet, skinless with bones removed	2 pounds
Olive Oil	3 tablespoons
Prepared Horseradish	1 tablespoon
Soy Sauce	1 tablespoon
Lemon Juice	1 tablespoon
Salt and White Pepper	as needed
Sour Cream	¾ cup
Mayonnaise	½ cup
Prepared Horseradish	2 tablespoons
Fresh Basil, chopped	1 tablespoon
Lemon Juice	1 tablespoon
Tabasco Sauce	1 teaspoon

Preparation

1. Cut the salmon into 5 evenly sized pieces about 1" thick. Preheat the grill to medium high heat.

2. Whisk together the oil, horseradish, soy sauce and lemon juice. Season each piece of fish generously with salt and white pepper then brush with the oil mixture. Grill until the center is just opaque about 4 minutes per side.

3. Mix together the sour cream, mayonnaise, horseradish, basil, lemon juice and Tabasco sauce. When the fish is finished on the grill, remove and place on a serving tray. Spread a small amount of the sour cream mixture on each piece of fish and serve immediately.

Honey Mustard Glazed Salmon

Ingredients

Salmon Filet, skinless with bones removed	1 each, about 3 pounds
Dry White Wine	1 cup
Butter, ½" cubes	½ cup
Dijon Mustard	⅔ cup
Whole Grain Mustard	⅓ cup
Honey	½ cup
Brown Sugar	½ cup
Dill Weed, dry	1 tablespoon

Preparation

1. Preheat oven to 350°.

2. Boil the wine and butter in a small sauce pot for three minutes. Season the salmon on all sides with salt and white pepper. Place onto a baking sheet with the skin side down. Pour the wine mixture over the fish and bake until opaque in the center, about 15 minutes.

3. Preheat the broiler. Drain the liquid from the pan and then mix together the mustards, honey, brown sugar, and dill weed. Spread over the salmon and broil until the topping is browned and bubbling, about 3 minutes. Transfer to a platter and serve immediately.

Sesame Salmon

Ingredients

Salmon, skinless with bones removed	2 pounds
Flour	2 cups
Ginger, ground	1 tablespoon
Garlic Powder	1 tablespoon
Onion Powder	1 tablespoon
Milk	2 cups
Eggs	4 each
Panko Bread Crumbs	4 cups
Sesame Seeds	1 cup

Preparation

1. Cut the salmon into evenly sized pieces about 1" wide, 3" long and ½" thick. Refrigerate.

2. Mix the flour, ginger, garlic powder and onion powder together and place into a pie plate or shallow pan. Pour the milk and eggs into a second pan and mix well with a fork. Stir together the bread crumbs and sesame seeds and put into a third pan. Take a piece of fish and gently coat it in the flour and carefully shake off any excess, then dip into the milk mixture and drain any excess before coating with the bread crumbs. Place the breaded fish onto a tray and repeat with the remaining pieces of fish.

3. Add the vegetable oil to a pot until about 1½ inches deep. Heat over medium to medium high heat until hot but not smoking. Add a few pieces of the breaded fish and fry until golden brown, turning occasionally to ensure even cooking, remove with tongs and drain on a paper towel. Season with salt while still hot. Cover the cooked fish loosely with a piece of foil while continuing to fry the remaining pieces.

4. Serve with Chili Aioli (page 171).

Chef TJ Weston

Simple Grilled Salmon

Ingredients

Salmon Filet, bones removed	1 each, about 3 pounds
White Wine	1 cup
Olive Oil	½ cup
Sugar	¼ cup
Lemon Pepper	1 tablespoon
Butter, melted	½ cup
Fresh Dill, chopped	1 tablespoon
Salt	as needed

Preparation

1. Cut the salmon into 6 equal pieces. Whisk together the wine, oil, sugar and lemon pepper. Pour the marinade over the salmon and refrigerate for 1 – 4 hours. Drain and pat the salmon dry with paper towels.

2. Preheat the grill to medium high heat and coat liberally with non-stick spray. Season the salmon with salt and place on the grill skin side up. Cook for 3 minutes, rotate 45° and cook for 3 more minutes.

3. Mix the butter and dill together. Flip the fish and brush with the dill butter. Continue cooking until the center is opaque, about 5 minutes. Brush with more butter and place the fish onto a platter and serve immediately.

Slow Roasted Salmon with Red Wine Glaze

Ingredients

Salmon Filet, bones removed	1 each, about 3 pounds
Red Wine	2 cups
Soy Sauce	1 cup
Brown Sugar	1 cup
Balsamic Vinegar	½ cup
Garlic, chopped	¼ cup
Ginger, chopped	¼ cup
Salt and White Pepper	as needed

Preparation

1. Place the wine, soy sauce, brown sugar, vinegar, garlic and ginger into a heavy pot and bring to a boil over high heat, stirring often. Reduce heat and simmer until thick and syrupy, and reduced by two thirds, about 1 – 1½ hours. Strain into a bowl and allow it to cool at room temperature.

2. Preheat the oven to 250°.

3. Season the salmon with salt and pepper. Brush with some of the glaze and let rest for 15 minutes, brush again and place in the oven. Cook until the center is opaque, about 45 minutes. Continue brushing with the glaze every 10 minutes while cooking. Remove from oven.

4. Preheat broiler.

5. Brush the remaining glaze onto the salmon and broil until golden with a shiny glaze, about 3 minutes. Transfer to a platter and serve.

Teriyaki Salmon

Ingredients

Salmon Filet, bones removed	1 each, about 3 pounds
White Wine	2 cups
Soy Sauce	2 cups
Brown Sugar	3 cups
Garlic, chopped	½ cup
Ginger, chopped	½ cup
Green Onion, white parts only, chopped	½ cup
Salt and White Pepper	as needed
Cilantro, chopped	¼ cup
Sesame Seeds	2 tablespoons

Preparation

1. Place the wine, soy sauce, brown sugar, garlic and ginger into a heavy pot and bring to a boil over high heat, stirring often. Reduce heat and simmer for 10 minutes. Pour half of the sauce into a bowl and allow to cool before chilling in the refrigerator. This will be the marinade for the salmon. Continue to simmer the other half remaining in the pot until reduced by one half. Strain and chill as well, this will be the sauce.

2. Preheat the broiler.

3. Cut the salmon into six equal pieces and place into the marinade. Allow to marinate for 1 – 4 hours, drain and pat dry with paper towels. Season with salt and white pepper and place onto a foil lined baking pan. Coat each piece with a little bit of the sauce.

4. Broil the salmon until it flakes easily when tested with a fork, about 5 – 7 minutes. Continue basting the fish with the sauce a few times as it cooks. Remove and transfer to a serving platter.

5. Sprinkle the cilantro and sesame seeds over each piece and serve.

Tortilla Salmon with Chipotle Mayonnaise

Ingredients

Salmon, skinless with bones removed	2 pounds
Flour	2 cups
Cumin	2 tablespoons
Paprika	1 tablespoon
Milk	2 cups
Eggs	4 each
Tortilla Chips, crushed	6 cups
Mayonnaise	1½ cups
Canned Chipotle Pepper	2 each
Lime, juiced	1 each
Cilantro, chopped	½ cup
Sugar	1 teaspoon

Chef TJ Weston

Preparation

1. Cut the salmon into evenly sized pieces about 1" wide, 3" long and ½" thick. Refrigerate.

2. Mix the flour, cumin and paprika together and place into a pie plate or shallow pan. Pour the milk and eggs into a second pan and mix well with a fork. Chop the tortilla chips in a food processor or crush by hand until very fine, put into a third pan. Take a piece of fish and gently coat it in the flour and carefully shake off any excess, then dip into the milk mixture and drain any excess before coating with the tortilla crumbs. Place the breaded fish onto a tray and repeat with the remaining pieces of fish.

3. Add the vegetable oil to a pot until about 1½ inches deep. Heat over medium to medium high heat until hot but not smoking. Add a few pieces of the breaded fish and fry until golden brown, turning occasionally to ensure even cooking, remove with tongs and drain on a paper towel. Season with salt while still hot. Cover the cooked fish loosely with a piece of foil while continuing to fry the remaining pieces.

4. To make the chipotle mayonnaise use a blender or food processor to puree the mayonnaise, chipotle pepper, lime juice, cilantro and sugar until very smooth. Pour into a small bowl and serve with the salmon.

MEATS

Having grown up in the Midwest I was raised on a hearty diet of beef, pork, and chicken and still enjoy preparing and eating the various proteins that the land has to offer. There are lots of ways to season and flavor meats from spice rubs to brines, injections and marinades but sticking to basic cooking techniques and being able to accurately judge the doneness are all it takes to prepare juicy, flavorful centerpieces to any meal.

Bacon Wrapped Turkey Breast

Ingredients

Turkey Breast, boneless	1 each, about 3 pounds
Basic Brine, page 164	1 gallon
Rosemary, ground	2 teaspoons
Bacon, thick sliced	1 – 2 pounds, as needed
Heavy Cream	2 cups
Honey	½ cup
Dijon Mustard	¼ cup
Salt and Pepper	as needed

Preparation

1. Remove the skin from the turkey and place in a large plastic container and cover with the brine. Refrigerate for 4 – 8 hours. Drain and pat dry with paper towels.

2. Preheat the oven to 400°.

3. Season the turkey breast on all sides with salt and pepper. Lay the bacon on a work surface so that the edges of each slice overlap just a little, using enough slices to extend the length of the entire turkey breast. Place the meat on one side of the loose ends of the bacon and carefully roll to wrap tightly with the bacon. Trim off the bacon when necessary so as not to use more than what is needed to create one wrap around the turkey that overlaps by about 1" on the underside.

4. Transfer to a rack placed on a roasting pan and roast in the oven rotating occasionally to ensure even browning. Cook to an internal temperature of 165°, about 1 hour. Remove and cover loosely with a piece of foil. Allow to rest for 10 minutes.

5. In a heavy sauce pot add the heavy cream, honey, Dijon mustard and season with salt and pepper. Simmer over medium high heat until thick and reduced by about one half.

6. Slice the turkey into thin pieces and arrange neatly on a serving platter. Drizzle with the sauce and serve immediately.

Bangkok Broil

Ingredients

Flank Steak	3 pounds
Soy Sauce	½ cup
Honey	½ cup
Worcestershire Sauce	¼ cup
White Wine	¼ cup
Ketchup	¼ cup
Ginger, chopped	¼ cup
Garlic, chopped	¼ cup
Green Onion, white parts only, chopped	¼ cup
Limes, juiced	2 each
Chili Sauce, Sriracha Brand	1 tablespoon
Salt and Black Pepper	as needed
Limes, cut into wedges	3 each
Cilantro, leaves picked	½ cup

Preparation

1. Trim all of the fat and sinew from the beef, leaving ¼" cap of fat on the top. This will help to keep the meat juicy while cooking. Place the trimmed meat into a large bowl.

2. In a blender puree together the soy sauce, honey, Worcestershire sauce, white wine, ketchup, ginger, garlic, green onion, lime juice and chili sauces. Mix until well blended but not completely smooth. Pour over the beef and stir to mix well. Refrigerate for 4 – 12 hours.

3. Preheat the broiler to high.

4. Drain the marinade from the beef and season generously with salt and pepper. Place onto a rack inside of a roasting pan with the fat side up. Broil until lightly browned and cooked to desired doneness, turning once during cooking. About 4 minutes per side.

5. Remove and transfer to a plate, cover loosely with foil. Let rest for ten minutes. Slice very thinly against the grain and arrange neatly on a platter. Serve with lime wedges and cilantro leaves.

BBQ Baby Back Ribs

Ingredients

Baby Back Ribs	4 racks
BBQ Dry Rub, page 165	1 cup
Traditional Barbeque Sauce, page 166	4 cups

Preparation

1. Rinse the ribs under cold running water and pat dry with paper towels. Place one rack on a baking sheet and season both sides generously with the dry rub, repeat with the remaining racks. Cover with plastic wrap and refrigerate for 1 – 2 days.

2. Line the bottom of the oven with foil to create a tray to catch any drippings. Preheat the oven to 250°.

3. Brush each rack on both sides with the barbeque sauce. Place directly onto the oven rack and cook until tender, but not falling apart, about 2½ - 3 hours. Remove from oven and brush with more sauce.

4. Preheat the grill to medium high heat with a few handfuls of wood chips. Once very smoky cook the ribs with the lid down until slightly charred, about 4 minutes per side. Remove the ribs from the grill and brush with more sauce. Serve immediately.

Carolina Style BBQ Pork

Ingredients

Pork Butt, boned and tied	3 pounds
BBQ Dry Rub, page #	1 cup
Chicken Stock	3 cups
Liquid Smoke	2 tablespoons
Cider Vinegar	1½ cups
Water	½ cup
Sugar	¼ cup
Onion, chopped	1 each
Cayenne Pepper, ground	1 teaspoon
Carolina BBQ sauce, page 167	1 cup
Salt and Pepper	as needed

Preparation

1. Place the pork into a large roasting pan and season all over with the BBQ Dry Rub. Add the chicken stock and liquid smoke to the pan. Cover with several sheets of parchment paper and aluminum foil, seal tightly.

2. Cook in the oven until very tender or with an internal temperature of 195°. About 6 hours. Remove and transfer the pork to a plate and cover loosely with a piece of foil, let rest for 15 minutes.

3. In a small bowl stir together the cider vinegar, water, sugar, onion and cayenne pepper. Set aside.

4. Pull off and discard any fat from the meat and then use two forks to shred the pork. Place in a bowl and stir in the vinegar mixture and season with salt and pepper. Transfer to a platter and serve with the Carolina BBQ sauce on the side.

Grilled Pork Chops with Pineapple Chutney

Ingredients

Pork Chops, 2-3" thick	6 each
Basic Brine, page 164	4 cups
Olive Oil	4 tablespoons
Salt and Black Pepper	as needed
Grilling Juice, page 168	½ cup
Red Pepper, chopped	1 each
Onion, chopped	1 each
Garlic, minced	1 tablespoon
Canned Pineapple, chunks	1 can (14.5 ounces)
Brown Sugar	½ cup
Rice Vinegar	½ cup

Preparation

1. Rinse the pork off under cold water and place in a bowl. Cover with the brine and refrigerate for 30 minutes. Drain and season with 2 tablespoons of olive oil, salt and pepper.

2. In a heavy pot heat the remaining olive oil over medium high heat. Once smoking add the red pepper, onion and garlic. Cook, stirring often, until tender and slightly charred. Add the pineapple and cook for a few minutes to dry off most of the juice. Add the brown sugar and rice vinegar. Reduce heat and simmer until thick and syrupy, about 30 minutes. Season with salt and pepper, cover and set aside.

3. Preheat the grill.

4. Grill the pork chops over medium heat, basting with the grilling juice about every five minutes. Cook until chops are just slightly pink in the very center or a thermometer reads 155°. About8 - 10 minutes per side. Remove and let rest on a plate loosely covered with foil for 5 minutes.

5. Transfer to a platter and top with the pineapple chutney. Serve immediately.

Grilled Beef Tri-Tip Steak with Tomato Relish

Ingredients

Tri-Tip Steak	3 pounds
Olive Oil	½ cup
Garlic, chopped	¼ cup
Red Wine Vinegar	¼ cup
Parsley, chopped	¼ cup
Black Pepper, ground	2 teaspoons
Cherry Tomatoes, halved	2 cups
Parsley, chopped	½ cup
Extra Virgin Olive Oil	¼ cup
Lemon, juiced	1 each
Garlic, chopped	1 tablespoon
Salt and Black Pepper	as needed

Preparation

1. Trim all fat and sinew from the beef, place into a plastic container. Using a food processor pulse together the olive oil, garlic, vinegar, parsley and black pepper. Pour over the meat, mix well, and refrigerate for 4 – 8 hours.

2. In a bowl gently stir together the tomatoes, parsley, extra virgin olive oil, lemon juice and garlic. Season with salt and black pepper, set aside.

3. Preheat the grill to medium high heat.

4. Drain the meat and pat dry with paper towels, season all sides with salt and pepper and rub with a little olive oil. Grill on each side, rotating often, about 7 minutes for medium rare and 10 for medium.

5. Transfer to a plate and cover loosely with foil, allow to rest for 10 minutes before slicing. Slice the meat into thin pieces and arrange neatly on a platter. Spoon the relish down the center of the meat and serve immediately.

Herb Roasted Chicken

Ingredients

Whole Chicken	2 each (3 pounds each)
Lemon, cut in ¼'s	2 each
Parsley	1 bunch
Bay Leaves	4 each
Olive oil	¼ cup
Thyme, dried	1 tablespoon
Rosemary, ground	2 teaspoons
Salt and Black Pepper	as needed
Cornstarch	1 teaspoon
Sherry, or other liquid	2 teaspoons

Preparation

1. Preheat the oven to 450°.

2. Remove the innards from each chicken and rinse well under cold running water. Season the inside with salt and pepper and then stuff with four lemon pieces and half of the parsley and bay leaves.

3. Drizzle the chickens with the olive oil and sprinkle with the thyme, rosemary, salt and pepper. Rub gently to evenly coat the entire surface. Fold the wings back and truss tightly using butcher's twine.

4. Place onto a rack inside of a roasting pan. Cook for ten minutes, turn the heat down to 350°, and continue cooking until the juices are clear and a thermometer inserted in the thigh reads 160°, about 45 minutes.

5. Remove and allow the chickens to rest loosely covered with foil. Pour the juices from the pan into a sauce pot and bring to a simmer over medium high heat. Simmer for a few minutes, carefully skimming any fat and solids that rise to the surface. In a small bowl mix together the cornstarch and sherry, slowly whisk into the pot and bring back to a simmer. Remove from heat and season as needed.

6. Carve the chickens into six pieces; two breasts, two thighs, and two legs. Place on a platter and serve with the sauce on the side.

Roasted Pork Loin with Mustard Cream Sauce

Ingredients

Pork Loin, center cut	3 pounds
Basic Brine, page 164	4 cups
Olive Oil	4 tablespoons
Onion, minced	1 each
White Wine	½ cup
Dijon Mustard	¼ cup
Whole Grain Mustard	2 tablespoons
Honey	2 tablespoons
Heavy Cream	2 cups
Salt and Black Pepper	as needed

Preparation

1. Trim all fat and sinew from the pork loin and place in a pan, cover with the brine and refrigerate for 4 – 8 hours. Drain and pat dry with paper towels. Season all sides with salt and pepper.

2. Preheat the oven to 375°.

3. Heat three tablespoons of the olive oil in a large skillet over high heat. Once smoking, add the pork loin and sear each side until very golden. About 2 minutes per side. Remove and transfer to a rack on a roasting pan. Roast in the oven until a thermometer inserted in the center reads 155°, about 45 minutes. Remove and cover loosely with foil.

4. In a heavy pot heat the remaining tablespoon of olive oil over medium high heat. When hot but not smoking add the onions and cook until tender but with no color, about 3 minutes. Add the wine, mustards and honey. Simmer until almost all of the liquid has evaporated. Add the heavy cream and simmer until reduced by one half. Remove from heat, season with salt and pepper.

5. Slice the pork into very thin pieces and arrange on a platter. Drizzle with the sauce and serve immediately.

Sautéed Skirt Steak with Mushrooms and Onions

Ingredients

Skirt Steak	5 pounds
Beef Marinade, page 182	2 cups
Olive Oil	2 tablespoons
Mushrooms, cut in ¼'s	1 pound
Onion, diced	1 each
Sherry	¼ cup
Steak Butter, page 169	¼ cup
Parsley, chopped	1 tablespoon
Salt and Black Pepper	as needed

Preparation

1. Trim all fat and sinew from the skirt steaks and cut into 4" lengths, place in a bowl and cover with the marinade. Refrigerate for 1 – 4 hours. Drain and pat dry with paper towels. Season all sides with salt and pepper.

2. Heat the olive oil in a large skillet over high heat until smoking. Add a few pieces of the meat and cook until well browned, flip and repeat, about 2 minutes per side. Transfer to a plate and cover loosely with foil, repeat with the remaining pieces of meat.

3. Once all of the meat has been cooked and placed onto the plate, add the mushrooms and onions to the pan. Season with salt and pepper and cook until tender and golden brown, about 5 minutes. Carefully add the sherry and reduce the heat to medium. Once most of the liquid has evaporated add the steak butter and parsley. Gently swirl the pan to mix everything, remove from heat.

4. Transfer the meat to a serving platter and top with the mushrooms and onions. Spoon some of the sauce over each piece. Serve immediately.

SIDE DISHES

These are what make the meal complete and sometimes are often considered the best part. Everyone eats turkey on Thanksgiving but when asked about the dinner they usually talk about the candied yams or the green bean casserole and that is because those side dishes define the meal. No matter how great the hamburgers or chicken might be it is the coleslaw or potato salad and baked beans that make it a barbecue and that is why good side dishes can turn an ordinary dinner into a memorable feast.

Steamed Broccoli with Cheddar Sauce

Ingredients

Broccoli Bunches	2 ponds
Butter	½ cup
Flour	½ cup
Milk, hot	2 cups
Mustard Powder	½ teaspoon
Salt	½ teaspoon
White Pepper	¼ teaspoon
Cheddar Cheese, grated	2 cups

Preparation

1. Cut the florets from the broccoli stems, leaving large bite size pieces. Place in a steamer basket in a pot with 1" of boiling water. Cover and cook over high heat until tender, about 5 – 7 minutes.

2. While broccoli is steaming, melt the butter over medium high heat in a sauce pan. Add the flour and whisk for 1 minute, making sure it does not brown. Add the milk, mustard powder, salt and white pepper. Continue cooking and stirring constantly until simmering.

3. Reduce heat and stir in the cheese. Whisk until smooth, remove from heat and serve immediately.

Corn on the Cob

Ingredients

Ears of Corn	6 each
Milk	2 cups
Sugar	½ cup
Salt	¼ cup
Butter	¼ cup

Preparation

1. Clean the corn by peeling away the husks and silk strings. Place into a large pot and add all remaining ingredients. Add enough cold water to just cover the corn by about 1". Cover and bring to a boil over medium high heat. Reduce heat and simmer until the corn is tender, about 10 minutes.

2. Remove from heat and let rest until ready to serve. Drain and serve immediately.

Creamed Peas with Bacon and Onion

Ingredients

Peas, frozen	2 pounds
Bacon, chopped	½ pound
Onion, diced	1 each
Flour	¼ cup
Milk, hot	2 cups
Salt and White Pepper	as needed

Preparation

1. Put the bacon in a heavy bottomed pot and cook over medium high heat until it begins to brown. Add the onion and cook stirring often until tender, about 2 minutes. Drain off about half of the fat and add the flour, stirring constantly for 1 minute, making sure it does not brown. Add the milk and season with the salt and white pepper. Continue cooking and stirring constantly until simmering and begins to thicken. Remove from heat.

2. Bring a large pot of water to a rolling boil over high heat. Add ¼ cup of salt and the peas. Boil uncovered until tender, about 7 minutes. Strain and return to the pot.

3. Add the cream sauce and stir gently. Cook for a few minutes, stirring occasionally. Season with salt and white pepper as needed and serve immediately.

Garlic Mashed Potatoes

Ingredients

Idaho Potatoes, peeled	3 pounds
Garlic, peeled	12 cloves
Heavy Cream, hot	1 cup
Sour Cream	1 cup
Butter, room temperature	½ cup
Nutmeg, ground	¼ teaspoon
Salt and White Pepper	as needed

Preparation

1. Cut the potatoes in half and place into a large pot with the garlic cloves. Cover with cold water to about 1" above the potatoes, add ¼ cup of salt and cover with a lid. Bring to a boil over high heat.

2. Cook the potatoes until tender, adjust the temperature as needed to prevent the water from boiling over, about 45 minutes. Strain and return to the pot.

3. Add the remaining ingredients and begin mashing with either a hand masher or an electric mixer. Adjust the consistency with additional cream, and taste for seasoning.

Green Beans with Almonds and Brown Butter

Ingredients

Green Beans, trimmed	2 pounds
Almonds, sliced	1 cup
Butter	½ cup
Salt and Black Pepper	as needed

Preparation

1. Preheat the oven to375°.

2. Place the almonds on a baking sheet and spread into one even layer. Place in the oven on the middle rack and cook until lightly toasted, stirring occasionally, about 5 – 7 minutes.

3. Melt the butter in a sauce pot over medium high heat and continue to simmer until light brown and has a toasted aroma. Pour into a bowl.

4. Bring a large pot of water to a boil over high heat. Add ¼ cup of salt. Put the green beans in and cook uncovered until tender, about 10 minutes. Drain and return to the pot.

5. Add the almonds, browned butter, salt and black pepper to the green beans and stir gently. Serve immediately.

Chef TJ Weston

Ginger Glazed Carrots

Ingredients

Carrots, peeled	8 each
Butter	¼ cup
Ginger, peeled and minced	2 teaspoons
Honey	¼ cup
Chicken Stock	¼ cup
Salt and White Pepper	as needed

Preparation

1. In a sauce pan melt the butter over medium high heat. Add the ginger and cook, stirring occasionally for 2 minutes. Add the honey, chicken stock, salt and white pepper. Allow to simmer until reduced by one half. Remove from heat.

2. Cut each carrot into thirds. Cut the thickest piece into quarters lengthwise, the center piece in half and the tip end can be left whole. Bring a large pot of water to a rolling boil over high heat. Add ¼ cup of salt and the carrots. Cook until tender, about 5 minutes.

3. Strain the carrots and return back to the pot along with the ginger glaze. Simmer over high heat while stirring for 1 – 2 minutes, or until the glaze reduces and coats the carrots. Serve immediately.

Macaroni and Cheese

Ingredients

Macaroni, elbow or shell noodles	1 pound
Butter	½ cup
Onion, minced	¼ cup
Flour	½ cup
Milk, hot	4 cups
Dijon Mustard	2 teaspoons
Tabasco Sauce	½ teaspoon
Salt and White Pepper	as needed
Cheddar Cheese, grated	4 cups
Bread Crumbs	1 cup

Preparation

1. Preheat oven to 350°.

2. Bring a large pot of water to a rolling boil over high heat. Add ¼ cup of salt, then stir in the macaroni. Cook, stirring often, until tender, about 7 minutes. Strain.

3. Melt the butter over medium high heat in a sauce pan. Add the onion and cook stirring often until tender but with no color, about 2 minutes. Add the flour and whisk for 1 minute, making sure it does not brown. Add the milk, mustard, Tabasco sauce, salt and white pepper. Continue cooking and stirring constantly until simmering, remove from heat and stir in the cheese.

4. In a large bowl stir together the pasta and the cheese sauce. Pour into a casserole dish and sprinkle with the bread crumbs. Bake until hot and bubbling and the crumbs begin to brown, about 20 – 30 minutes. If necessary finish by broiling the bread crumbs to get a nice golden crust.

Mashed Butternut Squash

Ingredients

Butternut Squash, large	2 each
Butter, melted	2 tablespoons
Brown Sugar	2 tablespoons
Salt and White Pepper	as needed
Heavy Cream, hot	¼ cup
Salt	½ teaspoon
Nutmeg	½ teaspoon
White Pepper	¼ teaspoon
Butter, room temperature	¼ cup

Preparation

1. Preheat the oven to 400°.

2. Cut the squash in half lengthwise and remove the seeds with a spoon. Place in a pan, cut side up, and drizzle with the melted butter. Sprinkle the brown sugar, salt and white pepper over the entire surface and roast until tender, about 45 minutes.

3. While the squash is warm, scoop out the flesh with a spoon into a pot. Add the heavy cream, salt, nutmeg and white pepper. Mash with a potato masher or electric mixer, then cook over medium heat until almost dry, about 5 minutes.

4. Remove from heat and stir in the butter. Adjust seasoning as needed. Keep covered until ready to serve.

Rosemary Roasted Potatoes

Ingredients

Red Bliss Potatoes, washed	3 pounds
Olive Oil	¼ cup
Rosemary, chopped	2 tablespoons
Garlic, chopped	1 tablespoon
Red Pepper Flakes	1 teaspoon
Salt and Black Pepper	as needed

Preparation

1. Preheat the oven to 450°. Cut each potato in to quarters lengthwise.

2. In a bowl toss together all of the ingredients and season with salt and black pepper. Pour onto a baking pan and arrange in one even layer.

3. Roast until golden brown and tender, stirring occasionally, about 25 -30 minutes.

Traditional Coleslaw

Ingredients

Mayonnaise	1 cup
Dijon Mustard	1 tablespoon
Olive Oil, extra virgin	1 tablespoon
Lemon, juiced	1 each
Red Wine Vinegar	2 tablespoons
Sugar	¼ cup
Green Cabbage, shredded	1 head
Red Cabbage, shredded	¼ head
Carrot, shredded	1 each
Zucchini, seeded and shredded	1 each
Red Pepper, sliced thin	1 each
Yellow Pepper, sliced thin	1 each
Red Onion, sliced thin	1 each
Celery Seed	1 tablespoon
Salt and Black Pepper	as needed

Preparation

1. In a mixing bowl whisk together the mayonnaise, mustard, olive oil, lemon juice, vinegar and sugar. Cover and refrigerate.

2. In a large bowl gently toss together all of the vegetables, and celery seed. Add enough of the dressing to just lightly coat everything, season with salt and black pepper. Cover and refrigerate for at least 2 hours before serving.

Zucchini Gratin

Ingredients

Olive Oil	¼ cup
Yellow Zucchini	4 each
Green Zucchini	4 each
Onion, diced	1 each
Corn Kernels, fresh or frozen	1½ cups
Garlic, chopped	6 cloves
Tomatoes	3 each
Basil, dried	2 teaspoons
Butter	½ cup
Flour	½ cup
Milk, hot	2 cups
Nutmeg, ground	¼ teaspoon
Salt and White Pepper	as needed
Swiss Cheese, grated	2 cups
Bread Crumbs	1 cup

Preparation

1. Preheat oven to 400°.

2. Cut the ends off of the zucchini and split in half lengthwise, cut again to quarter each half. Carefully cut out the seeds and then cut into ½" dice. Do the same to the tomatoes but keep separate.

3. Heat the olive oil in a large skillet over medium high heat. Once the oil begins to smoke, add both types of zucchini and the onion. Sauté until tender, about 5 minutes. Add the corn and garlic and continue cooking for 2 more minutes. Add the tomatoes and basil then season with salt and white pepper. Remove from heat and drain the vegetables in a large colander to remove any excess moisture created while cooking.

4. Melt the butter over medium high heat in a sauce pan. Add the flour and whisk for 1 minute, making sure it does not brown. Add the milk, nutmeg, salt and white pepper. Continue cooking and stirring constantly until simmering, remove from heat and stir in the cheese.

5. In a large bowl stir together the vegetables and the cheese sauce. Pour into a casserole dish and sprinkle with the bread crumbs. Bake until hot and bubbling and the crumbs begin to brown, about 20 – 30 minutes. If necessary finish by broiling the bread crumbs to get a nice golden crust.

Twice Baked Potatoes

Ingredients

Idaho Potatoes, scrubbed clean	8 each
Bacon, chopped	¼ pound
Sour Cream	1 cup
Cheddar Cheese, grated	1 cup + extra
Green Onion, green part only, chopped	2 each
Salt and White Pepper	to taste

Preparation

1. Preheat the oven to 400°.

2. Place the bacon in a heavy pot and cook over medium high heat until golden brown, stirring often. Remove and drain on paper towels.

3. Stab each potato a few times with a fork and bake in the oven until tender, about 45 minutes. While still warm, cut a small piece off of the top of each potato and use a spoon to scoop out the flesh into a bowl. Remove as much flesh as possible and be careful not to tear the skins. Reserve six of the skins, the other two will only be used for the filling.

4. Using a hand masher or electric mixer, mix the potato, bacon, sour cream, cheddar cheese, green onion, salt and white pepper. Once it is evenly mixed together, use a spoon to refill each potato skin. The filling should rise about ¼" above the top of the skin. Place in a baking pan and sprinkle the tops with a little extra cheddar cheese.

5. Bake potatoes until hot and the cheese on top is melted. About 10 minutes.

BREADS

Few things in life are better than fresh bread. I am not speaking about the spongy brick-like creature that comes out of those countertop machines that still remain trendy for reasons I will never even try to comprehend, but rather the type that is kneaded and shaped by hand before baking in an oven. The aroma alone is unrivaled by anything else that occurs in the kitchen and the ability to bake a good loaf of bread is an honorable talent, but with a simple recipe and some practice anyone can make first-rate breads at home.

Classic White Bread

Ingredients

Warm Water, 105°-115°	¾ cup
Yeast, active dry	1 tablespoon
Sugar	1 teaspoon
Buttermilk, room temperature	1 ½ cups
Butter, melted	2 tablespoons
Honey	3 tablespoons
Salt	1 tablespoon
Flour	6½ - 7 cups
Egg Yolk	1 each
Water, cold	1 tablespoon

Preparation

1. Pour the warm water in a small bowl. Sprinkle the yeast and sugar over the surface of the water, stir and let stand at room temperature until foamy, about 10 minutes.

2. In a large bowl, add the yeast mixture, buttermilk, butter, honey, salt and half of the flour. Mix with a wooden spoon until a soft dough is formed. Turn out onto the counter and begin kneading the dough, adding a ½ cup of flour at a time.

3. Once all of the flour has been added and the dough is just sticky enough to handle, continue kneading into soft and smooth dough, about 10 minutes.

4. Spray a bowl with non stick spray, add the dough and turn over to coat with the spray. Cover and let rest at room temperature until it is doubled in size, about 1 ½ hours.

5. Gently punch down the dough, turn onto the counter and cut into two equal pieces. Shape each piece into a loaf and place in a greased bread pan. Cover and let rest until doubled, about 1 hour.

6. Fifteen minutes before baking, preheat the oven to 375°. Beat the egg yolk and cold water together in a small bowl and brush lightly on each loaf. Bake for 35 – 45 minutes, or until nicely browned, pull away from the sides of the pan, and sound hollow when tapped with your finger. Cool completely on a rack before slicing.

Buttermilk Biscuits

Ingredients

Flour	5 cups
Baking Powder	4 teaspoons
Salt	1 tablespoon
Shortening, cold	½ cup
Buttermilk, cold	1 ½ cups
Butter, melted	3 tablespoons

Preparation

1. Preheat oven to 500°F with rack in middle.

2. Sift together flour, baking powder, and salt into a large bowl. Add butter, coating it with flour, then rub between your fingertips until coarsely blended with some ½-inch lumps still remaining.

3. Make a well in the flour mixture, add buttermilk and stir just until a dough forms (it will be soft and sticky). Turn dough out onto a floured surface and knead 8 to 10 times. Roll out dough with a floured rolling pin into a 12-inch round (1/2 inch thick) and, using a fork dipped in flour, prick all the way through about every 1/2 inch.

4. Cut out as many rounds as possible with a 2 1/2- to 3-inch round cookie/biscuit cutter or glass dipped in flour. Bake, almost touching, on an ungreased heavy baking sheet, rotating sheet after about 5 minutes if browning unevenly, until crusty and golden-brown, about 10 to 12 minutes. Brush tops with melted butter and serve warm.

Dinner Rolls

Ingredients

Warm Water, 105°-115°	½ cup
Yeast, active dry	2 tablespoon
Milk, room temperature	1 ½ cups
Sugar	½ cup
Salt	1 tablespoon
Egg	2 each
Butter, softened	½ cup
Flour	7 - 8 cups
Egg Yolk	1 each
Water, cold	1 tablespoon

Preparation

1. Pour the warm water in a small bowl. Sprinkle the yeast and a pinch of the sugar over the surface of the water, stir and let stand at room temperature until foamy, about 10 minutes.

2. In a large bowl, add the yeast mixture, milk, sugar, salt, eggs, butter and half of the flour. Mix with a wooden spoon until a soft dough is formed. Turn out onto the counter and begin kneading the dough, adding a ½ cup of flour at a time.

3. Once all of the flour has been added and the dough is just sticky enough to handle, continue kneading into a soft and smooth dough, about 10 minutes.

4. Spray a bowl with non stick spray, add the dough and turn over to coat the top. Cover and let rest at room temperature until it is doubled in size, about 1 ½ hours.

5. Gently punch down the dough, turn onto the counter and cut into 20 pieces. Shape each piece into a ball by rolling with your hands and then place on a greased baking sheet. Cover and let rest until doubled, about 30 minutes.

6. Fifteen minutes before baking, preheat the oven to 375°. Beat the egg yolk and cold water together in a small bowl and brush lightly on each dough ball. Bake for 15 – 20 minutes, or until nicely browned, and sound hollow when tapped with your finger. Cool on a rack.

French Bread

This dough is best made using a food processor because it is very wet and sticky. It can be done by hand if necessary, just use a little more flour.

Ingredients

Yeast, active dry	2 teaspoons
Warm Water, 105°-115°	1 2/3 cup
Flour	4 cups
Salt	1 ½ teaspoons
Vinegar, white	2 teaspoons
Olive Oil	1 tablespoon

Preparation

1. Put the yeast and water in a small bowl and stir to dissolve. Wait until foamy, about 10 minutes.

2. In the bowl of a food processor fitted with the blade attachment; add the flour, salt, and vinegar. Pulse several times to mix everything.

3. With motor running, slowly pour in the yeast mixture. Let the motor run until the dough ball just begins to clear the sides, about 1 minute. Cover the tube with plastic wrap and let rest for one hour.

4. Pulse a few times to deflate the dough. Turn out onto the counter and roll into a long, thin strand about 15" x 3". Place onto a greased baking sheet and drizzle with the olive oil. Let rest until almost doubled, about 45 minutes.

5. Twenty minutes before baking preheat the oven to 400°. Brush the dough lightly with warm water and bake for 25 – 35 minutes. The bread will be done when it is golden brown, and sounds hollow when tapped with your finger. Cool completely on a rack before slicing.

Herb Focaccia Bread

Ingredients

Warm Water, 105°-115°	½ cup
Yeast, active dry	1 teaspoon
Flour	¾ cup
Warm Water, 105°-115°	1 cup
Yeast, active dry	1 teaspoon
Olive Oil	¼ cup
Flour	3 ½ cups
Basil, dried	2 teaspoon
Oregano, dried	1 teaspoon
Salt	1 tablespoon

Preparation

1. Pour the ½ cup of warm water in a small bowl. Sprinkle 1 teaspoon of yeast and the ¾ cup of flour in to the water and mix well. Cover and let rest at room temperature until bubbly and doubled in bulk, about 2 hours.

2. In a large bowl, add the rest of the water and sprinkle in the remaining yeast. Stir and let rest until bubbly, about 10 minutes. Add the yeast mixture, olive oil, half of the flour, herbs and salt. Mix with a wooden spoon until a soft dough is formed. Turn out onto the counter and begin kneading the dough, adding a ½ cup of flour at a time.

3. Once all of the flour has been added and the dough is just sticky enough to handle, continue kneading into a soft and smooth dough, about 10 minutes.

4. Spray a bowl with non stick spray, add the dough and turn over to coat the top. Cover and let rest at room temperature until it is doubled in size, about 1 ½ hours.

5. Gently punch down the dough, turn onto the counter and shape into the size of the baking pan it will be cooked in; recommend 11" x 17". Place the dough into a greased baking pan and careful stretch and pull it to cover the entire bottom of the pan. Let rest for ten minutes and then continue stretching and pulling the dough until it just reaches the sides of the pan. Drizzle with additional olive oil then cover and let rest until doubled, about 1 hour.

6. Fifteen minutes before baking, preheat the oven to 425°. Bake for 25 – 30 minutes, or until nicely browned, and sounds hollow when tapped with your finger. Cool on a rack.

Vienna Bread

Ingredients

Warm Water, 105°-115°	1 cup
Yeast, active dry	2 tablespoons
Sugar	1 tablespoon
Whole Milk, 105°-115°	1 cup
Flour, all-purpose	2 cups
Salt	1¼ tablespoons
Butter, melted	4 tablespoons
Whole Wheat Flour	3 cups
Flour, all-purpose	2 cups
Egg	1 each
Water, cold	1 tablespoon
Sesame Seeds	2 tablespoons

Chef TJ Weston

Preparation

1. In a large bowl whisk together the warm water, yeast, sugar, milk and 2 cups of flour. Cover with plastic wrap and let rise at room temperature until foamy and doubled in size, about two hours.

2. In another large bowl add the yeast mixture, salt, butter and half of each flour. Beat with a wooden spoon for one minute, then begin adding the rest of the flours ½ cup at a time.

3. Turn the dough onto a counter and knead by hand for ten minutes or until smooth and springy, dusting with more wheat flour as needed.

4. Spray a bowl with non stick spray, add the dough and turn over to coat with the spray. Cover and let rest at room temperature until it is doubled in size, about 2 hours.

5. Gently punch down the dough, turn onto the counter and cut into two equal pieces. Shape each piece into a loaf and place in a greased bread pan. Cover and let rest until doubled, about 1 hour.

6. Fifteen minutes before baking, preheat the oven to 375°. Whisk together the egg and cold water, gently brush each loaf and sprinkle with sesame seeds. Bake for 35 – 45 minutes, or until nicely browned, pull away from the sides of the pan, and sound hollow when tapped with your finger. Cool completely on a rack before slicing.

Oatmeal Raisin Bread

Ingredients

Raisins	½ cup
Boiling Water	1 cup
Warm Water, 105°-115°	½ cup
Yeast, active dry	2 tablespoons
Sugar	1 teaspoon
Whole Milk, room temperature	2 cups
Old-Fashioned Rolled Oats, not quick cooking	1 cup
Honey	½ cup
Butter, melted	¼ cup
Salt	1 tablespoon
Whole Wheat Flour	3 cups
Flour, all purpose	2 cups
Egg	1 each
Water, cold	1 tablespoon

Preparation

1. Put the raisins into a small bowl and cover with the boiling water. Cover with plastic wrap and let rest for 30 minutes. Drain.

2. Pour the warm water in a small bowl. Sprinkle the yeast and sugar over the surface of the water, stir and let stand at room temperature until foamy, about 10 minutes.

3. In a large bowl add the raisins, yeast mixture, milk, oats, honey, butter, salt and half of each flour. Mix with a wooden spoon until a soft dough is formed. Turn out onto the counter and begin kneading the dough, adding a ½ cup of each flour at a time.

4. Once all of the flour has been added and the dough is just sticky enough to handle, continue kneading into a soft and smooth dough, about 10 minutes.

5. Spray a bowl with non stick spray, add the dough and turn over to coat with the spray. Cover and let rest at room temperature until it is doubled in size, about 1 ½ hours.

6. Gently punch down the dough, turn onto the counter and cut into two equal pieces. Shape each piece into a loaf and place in a greased bread pan. Cover and let rest until doubled, about 1 hour.

7. Fifteen minutes before baking, preheat the oven to 375°. Beat the egg and cold water together in a small bowl and brush lightly on each loaf and sprinkle with the oats. Bake for 35 – 45 minutes, or until nicely browned, pull away from the sides of the pan, and sound hollow when tapped with your finger. Cool completely on a rack before slicing.

Whole Wheat Bread

Ingredients

Warm Water, 105°-115°	3 cups
Powdered Milk, or Dry Buttermilk	1 cup
Yeast, active dry	2 tablespoons
Honey	¾ cup
Whole Wheat Flour	3 cups
Olive Oil	½ cup
Salt	1¼ tablespoons
Whole Wheat Flour	3½ cups
Flour, all-purpose	3 cups
Butter, melted	4 tablespoons

Preparation

1. In a large bowl whisk together the warm water, powdered milk, yeast, honey and 3 cups of whole wheat flour. Cover with plastic wrap and let rise at room temperature until foamy and doubled in size, about two hours.

2. In another large bowl add the oil, salt, half of each type of flour, and the yeast mixture. Beat with a wooden spoon for one minute, then begin adding the rest of the flours ½ cup at a time.

3. Turn the dough onto a counter and knead by hand for ten minutes or until smooth and springy, dusting with more wheat flour as needed.

4. Spray a bowl with non stick spray, add the dough and turn over to coat with the spray. Cover and let rest at room temperature until it is doubled in size, about 2 hours.

5. Gently punch down the dough, turn onto the counter and cut into two equal pieces. Shape each piece into a loaf and place in a greased bread pan. Cover and let rest until doubled, about 1 hour.

6. Fifteen minutes before baking, preheat the oven to 375°. Brush each loaf with the melted butter. Bake for 35 – 45 minutes, or until nicely browned, pull away from the sides of the pan, and sound hollow when tapped with your finger. Cool completely on a rack before slicing.

Wild Rice Molasses Bread

The only way to improve this bred might be to try adding a handful of chopped walnuts when mixing in the wild rice.

Ingredients

Warm Water, 105°-115°	1 ¼ cups
Yeast, active dry	2 tablespoon
Brown Sugar	2 teaspoons
Milk, 105°-115°	1 cup
Butter, melted	½ cup
Molasses	½ cup
Wild Rice, cooked	1 ½ cups
Salt	1 tablespoon
Whole Wheat Flour	3 cups
Flour	5 cups

Preparation

1. Pour the warm water in a small bowl. Sprinkle the yeast and brown sugar over the surface of the water, stir and let stand at room temperature until foamy, about 10 minutes.

2. In a large bowl, add the yeast mixture, milk, butter, molasses, wild rice, salt and half of each flour. Mix with a wooden spoon until a soft dough is formed. Turn out onto the counter and begin kneading the dough, adding a ¼ cup of each flour at a time.

3. Once all of the flour has been added and the dough is just sticky enough to handle, continue kneading into a soft and smooth dough, about 10 minutes.

4. Spray a bowl with non stick spray, add the dough and turn over to coat with the spray. Cover and let rest at room temperature until it is doubled in size, about 2 hours.

5. Gently punch down the dough, turn onto the counter and cut into two equal pieces. Shape each piece into a loaf and place in a greased bread pan. Cover and let rest until doubled, about 1 hour.

6. Fifteen minutes before baking, preheat the oven to 375°. Bake for 35 – 45 minutes, or until nicely browned, pull away from the sides of the pan, and sound hollow when tapped with your finger. Cool completely on a rack before slicing.

Zesty Corn Bread

Ingredients

Sugar	½ cup
Cornmeal	2 cups
Flour	2 cups
Baking Powder	2 tablespoons
Salt	1 tablespoon
Garlic Powder	½ teaspoon
White Pepper	¼ teaspoon
Eggs	2 each
Milk	2 cups
Vegetable Oil	½ cup
Green Pepper, chopped	½ cup
Onion, chopped	½ cup
Corn Kernels, frozen	½ cup
Cheddar Cheese, grated	½ cup

Preparation

1. Preheat oven to 400°. Spray two 9" pie pans with non-stick spray and then sprinkle with a little sugar, set aside.

2. In a large bowl whisk together the sugar, cornmeal, flour, baking powder, salt, garlic powder and white pepper. Add the milk, eggs, and vegetable oil. Stir just enough to incorporate all of the ingredients.

3. Using a rubber spatula gently fold in the green pepper, onion, corn and cheddar cheese. Pour batter into the prepared pans and bake until golden brown and tooth pick inserted in the center comes out clean, about 25 – 30 minutes.

Irish Soda Bread

Ingredients

Whole Wheat Flour	2 cups
Flour	2½ cups
Baking Soda	1 teaspoon
Salt	1 teaspoon
Buttermilk	2 cups

Preparation

1. Preheat oven to 450°. Spray a 9" pie pan with non-stick spray and then sprinkle with a little flour, set aside.

2. In a large bowl stir together the whole wheat flour, flour, baking soda, and salt. Make a well in the center and add the milk, gently fold just until a shaggy dough is formed.

3. Turn out the dough onto the counter and lightly dust with a little additional flour. Knead the dough a few times just until it forms a soft ball and then pat it down into a 2" thick disk. Gently place into the pan.

4. Use a serrated knife to cut a deep X into the dough and prick each quarter with a fork. Bake for twenty five minutes, reduce the oven temperature to 400° and continue baking until the bread is a deep golden color, about 30 minutes more.

5. Transfer the bread to a cooling rack and allow it to cool completely before slicing.

DESSERTS

Show me someone who does not enjoy dessert and I will show you a liar. I do not know if anyone actually ever said that but they should because a nice dessert and maybe a cup of coffee is the greatest way to end a meal. I admit that I do get a little bit of guilty pleasure while making desserts, what with the pies and cakes, fruit, chocolate, sugar and syrups, seriously what is there not to enjoy!

Apple Pie

Serve this warm with caramel sauce and vanilla ice cream, or even plain is just fine.

Ingredients for the Crust

Flour, chilled	3 cups
Sugar	¼ cup
Salt	1 teaspoon
Butter, cold	½ cup
Shortening, cold	⅓ cup
Ice Water	6 – 8 tablespoons

Ingredients for the Filling

Apples, assorted varieties	9 each
Lemon, juiced	1 each
Sugar	⅔ cup
Cinnamon, ground	1 tablespoon
Mace, ground	½ teaspoon
Nutmeg, ground	½ teaspoon
Salt	½ teaspoon
Butter, small pieces	2 tablespoons
Egg White	1 each

Preparation

1. Preheat oven to 450°.

2. Combine the flour, sugar, and salt in the bowl of a food processor fitted with the metal blade and sprinkle the butter and shortening over the ingredients. Cover and pulse a few times until small clumps begin to form. Add the iced water through the feed tube, 1 tablespoon at a time, pulsing quickly until the dough begins to form into a ball. Turn the dough out onto a sheet of plastic wrap and seal tightly. Refrigerate for 30 minutes.

3. Take the dough from the refrigerator and cut it into 2 pieces, one slightly bigger than the other. Wrap the smaller piece in plastic wrap and return to the refrigerator. Roll out the bigger piece on a lightly floured surface until it's slightly larger than the pie pan. Careful drape the dough over the pie pan and gently press against the bottom and sides. Leave about an inch of dough hanging over the sides of the pan and cut any excess away. Refrigerate the crust for at least 30 minutes before filling.

4. Peel, core, and thinly slice the apples into a large bowl, mix in the lemon juice. Sprinkle with sugar and cinnamon and then add the mace and nutmeg. Pour the apple mixture into the prepared pie shell. Mound toward the center and dot with the butter pieces.

5. Roll out the remaining pastry and carefully lay it over the apples. Seal the edges and cut vent holes. Whisk together the egg white and a tablespoon of cold water, brush over the surface of the pie. Place the pie pan on a baking sheet and cook in the middle of the oven for 10 minutes. Turn the oven down to 350° F. and continue to cook for about another hour, until the top crust is a beautiful golden brown. If the edges start to darken too much, cover with a ribbon of aluminum foil.

Bread Pudding with Rum Sauce

Ingredients for the Bread Pudding

Whole Milk	2½ cups
Heavy Cream	1 cup
Sugar	1 cup
Eggs	4 each
Egg Yolks	4 each
Vanilla Extract	1 tablespoon
Nutmeg, ground	¼ teaspoon
Salt	¼ teaspoon
White Bread, crusts removed	12 slices
Butter, room temperature	3 tablespoons
Dried Cranberries	½ cup

Preparation

1. Preheat oven to 350°.

2. Lightly butter an 11 x 7-inch glass baking dish. Combine milk, cream, sugar, eggs, egg yolks, vanilla, nutmeg, and salt in large bowl and whisk to blend well. Spread 1 side of each bread slice with butter. Arrange 6 slices, buttered side up, in single layer in the dish, trim to fit if necessary. Sprinkle with currants. Top with remaining bread slices, buttered side up. Pour custard over bread in dish. Let stand 15 minutes, occasionally pressing bread into custard.

3. Place pudding dish into a 13x9x2-inch metal baking pan. Pour enough hot water into pan to come halfway up sides of pudding dish. Place in oven. Bake pudding until set in center and golden on top, about 45 minutes. Remove pudding from water bath. Serve warm or at room temperature with warm caramel sauce.

Ingredients for the Rum Sauce

Dark Brown Sugar	1 pound
Heavy Cream	1¾ cups
Light Corn Syrup	1 cup
Dark Rum, Myer's	3 ounces

Preparation

1. Whisk all ingredients in heavy large saucepan to blend and continue whisking over medium-high heat until the sauce begins to boil. Reduce heat to medium-low. Simmer until sauce is thick enough to coat a spoon, whisking occasionally, about 30 minutes.

2. Remove from heat and set aside until ready to use.

Classic Cheesecake

Top each slice of cake with a spoonful of your favorite pie filling and a little whipped cream. Nothing beats cherries or blueberries in my opinion!

Ingredients for the Crust

Graham Crackers, finely ground	1½ cups
Butter, melted	5 tablespoons
Sugar	⅓ cup
Salt	¼ teaspoon

Preparation

1. Preheat oven to 350°.

2. Mix together all of the ingredients, add more butter or cracker crumbs as needed until it has the texture of wet sand. Gently press the crust into a pie pan, making it even across the bottom and up the entire sides.

3. Bake until lightly golden, about 10 minutes. Remove from oven and place on a rack to cool.

Ingredients for the Filling

Cream Cheese, softened	5 (8 oz.) packages
Sugar	1¾ cups
Flour	3 tablespoons
Orange, zested	1 each
Lemon, zested	1 each
Eggs	5 each
Egg Yolks	2 each
Vanilla	1 teaspoon

Preparation

1. Preheat the oven to 500°.

2. Beat together cream cheese, sugar, flour, and fruit zests with an electric mixer until smooth. Add eggs and yolks, 1 at a time, then vanilla, beating on low speed until each ingredient is incorporated and scraping the sides of the bowl often.

3. Pour filling into crust and bake in middle of oven for 10 minutes, or until puffed. Reduce temperature to 200°F and continue baking until cake is mostly firm when it is gently shaken, about 1 hour.

4. Chill cake, covered loosely, at least 4 hours. Bring to room temperature before slicing and serving.

Pumpkin Pie with Spiced Cream

Ingredients

Sugar	¾ cup
Cinnamon, ground	1 teaspoon
Salt	1 teaspoon
Ginger, ground	½ teaspoon
Mace, ground	½ teaspoon
Eggs	2 each
Canned Pumpkin	1 each (15 oz.)
Evaporated Milk	12 ounces
Heavy Cream	2 cups
Pie Dough, page 150	½ recipe

Preparation

1. Preheat oven to 425°.

2. Roll out the pie dough and line a 9-inch glass pie pan. Refrigerate until ready to fill and bake.

3. In a large bowl stir together the sugar, cinnamon, salt, ginger and mace. Add the eggs and beat well. Stir in the canned pumpkin and the evaporated milk.

4. Pour into the prepared pie crust and bake for 15 minutes. Reduce temperature to 350° and bake for an additional 45 minutes or until a knife inserted in the center comes out clean.

5. Transfer to a wire rack and let cool for a few hours before serving.

6. Whip the heavy cream with a little extra sugar and ground ginger. Serve on top of each slice.

Big Fat Chocolate Cake with Butter Cream Frosting

Ingredients for the Cake

Bittersweet Chocolate, chopped	4½ ounces
Coffee	2¼ cups
Sugar	4½ cups
Flour	3¾ cups
Cocoa Powder	2¼ cups
Baking Soda	1 tablespoon
Salt	2 teaspoons
Baking Powder	1¼ teaspoons
Eggs	5 each
Vegetable Oil	1 cup
Sour Cream	2¼ cups
Vanilla Extract	2 teaspoons

Preparation

1. Preheat oven to 350°.

2. In a small pot over medium heat, add the chocolate and coffee and stir occasionally until the chocolate is completely melted. Remove from heat and set aside.

3. Sift together the sugar, flour, cocoa powder, baking soda, salt and baking powder into a large bowl.

4. Whip the eggs in a large mixing bowl with an electric mixer on high speed until light and lemon colored, about 5 minutes. Add the vegetable oil, sour cream and vanilla, mix well. Add a third of the flour mixture and mix on medium speed just until incorporated. Add half of the coffee mixture, mix lightly, and continue adding the flour and coffee until everything has been incorporated.

5. Pour the batter into two 12" round cake pans and bake until a toothpick inserted into the center comes out clean, about 1 – 1½ hours. Transfer to wire racks to cool before removing from the pans. Decorate the cakes with the Butter Cream Frosting.

Ingredients for the Frosting

Powdered Sugar	27 ounces
Cocoa Powder	6 ounces
Bittersweet Chocolate, chopped	6 ounces
Butter, room temperature	2 pounds
Vanilla Extract	1 tablespoon
Coffee	1 tablespoon

Preparation

1. In a small bowl add the chocolate, vanilla, and coffee and microwave just until melted and smooth, set aside. Sift together the powdered sugar and cocoa powder into another bowl.

2. Using an electric mixer beat the butter in a large bowl until very light and almost white in color, about five minutes. Carefully mix in the chocolate mixture and the powdered sugar mixture, beat until smooth.

Chocolate Pudding with Cookies

Serve this by spooning some of the chilled pudding into a small glass, place a few cookies in it and top with a dollop of whip cream.

Ingredients for the Pudding:

Sugar	2 tablespoons
Cornstarch	2 tablespoons
Cocoa Powder, unsweetened	2 tablespoons
Salt	½ teaspoon
Whole Milk	1½ cups
Heavy Cream	¾ cup
Milk Chocolate, chopped	5 ounces
Vanilla Extract	2 teaspoons

Preparation

1. Whisk together the sugar, cornstarch, cocoa powder, and salt in a heavy saucepan. Gradually whisk in the milk and heavy cream. Bring to a boil over medium high heat, whisking constantly, then boil for two minutes.

2. Remove from heat and add the chocolate and vanilla, continue whisking until smooth. Transfer to a bowl and refrigerate. Cover with plastic wrap pressed against the surface after two hours, to prevent a skin from forming.

Ingredients for the Cookies:

Flour	2 cups
Baking Powder	½ teaspoon
Salt	½ teaspoon
Butter, softened	¾ cup
Sugar	1 cup
Egg, large	1 each
Cinnamon, ground	1 teaspoon
Vanilla Extract	1 teaspoon

Preparation

1. Preheat oven to 350°.

2. Whisk together flour, baking powder, and salt in a small bowl.

3. Beat together butter and sugar in a large bowl with an electric mixer at medium-high speed until pale and fluffy, about 3 minutes. Beat in egg, cinnamon and vanilla. Reduce speed to low, then add flour mixture and mix until just combined.

4. Roll the dough into 1½" balls and place onto lightly greased baking sheet, about 2" apart. Bake until lightly golden, rotating tray halfway through cooking, about 15 minutes total. Remove from oven and allow to cool before transferring to a rack to cool completely.

Raspberry Peach Cobbler

~Serve this warm with a scoop of vanilla ice cream on top!

Ingredients

Peaches, peeled and sliced	6 cups
Raspberries	2 cups
Brown Sugar	¼ cup
Cornstarch	2 tablespoons
Sugar	2 cups
Flour	3 cups
Salt	1 teaspoon
Baking Powder	1 tablespoon
Butter, cold	⅔ cup
Egg Yolks, lightly beaten	2 each

Preparation

1. Preheat oven to 375°.

2. Gently mix together the peaches, raspberries, brown sugar and cornstarch. Pour into a lightly buttered baking dish.

3. Whisk together the sugar, flour, salt and baking powder. Cut in the butter using a fork or pastry cutter until very crumbly. Stir in the egg yolks and mix well.

4. Sprinkle the topping over the fruit mixture being certain to cover any exposed fruit. Bake until golden brown and bubbling, about 30 minutes.

Chef TJ Weston

MISCELLANEOUS

I have always appreciated sauces, condiments and all of the other little tidbits that commonly grace the table. It is truly amazing what a few simple ingredients can become and what a role they can have with other foods from the way that a cucumber can be morphed into a pickle or how a lemon and a few cloves of garlic meld into a wonderful sauce. I often think that the more common and basic an item is the less appreciated it becomes and it should not be this way though because most of these items that we have come to know and expect have withstood the test of time and have defined our foods and the way we eat.

Basic Brine

This brine works well for pork and poultry and can be flavored with herbs and spices if you want.

Ingredients

Cold Water	1 gallon
Salt	1 cup
Brown Sugar	½ cup

Preparation

1. Place all of the ingredients in pot and bring to a boil over high heat. Stir well to dissolve everything.

2. Remove from heat and allow it to cool to room temperature then refrigerate until chilled.

BBQ Dry Rub

This spice mix is great as a dry rub for meats and fish before grilling but can also be used as a seasoning for barbecue sauces, beans, etcetera.

Ingredients

Salt	2 tablespoons
Brown Sugar	2 tablespoons
Black Pepper, ground	2 tablespoons
Celery Seed	2 tablespoons
Chili Powder	2 tablespoon
Paprika, smoked	1 tablespoon
Nutmeg, ground	1 tablespoon
Garlic Powder	1 tablespoon
Onion Salt	1 tablespoon
Marjoram, dried	1 tablespoon
Thyme, dried	1 tablespoon

Preparation

1. Place all of the ingredients in a bowl and mix well. Store in an airtight container in the freezer.

Traditional BBQ Sauce

This is a great sauce by itself or can be easily adapted to your preferences.

Ingredients

Ketchup	4 cups
Brown Sugar	½ cup
Cider Vinegar	½ cup
Molasses	¼ cup
Honey	¼ cup
Worcestershire Sauce	¼ cup
Whiskey	2 tablespoons
Yellow Mustard	2 tablespoons
Salt	1 tablespoon
Liquid Smoke	1 tablespoon
Chili Powder	1 tablespoon
Black Pepper, ground	2 teaspoons
Garlic Powder	2 teaspoons
Allspice	2 teaspoons

Preparation

1. Combine all the ingredients in a heavy sauce pan and bring to a boil over medium high heat.

2. Reduce heat and simmer until thick, about 15 – 20 minutes. Transfer to a plastic container, cool and then refrigerate.

Carolina Style BBQ Sauce

Here is my version of the tangy vinegar and mustard based sauces that characterize Carolina Barbeque.

Ingredients

White Vinegar	½ cup
Cider Vinegar	¼ cup
Chicken Stock	½ cup
Onion, chopped	½ cup
Jalapeno, seeded and minced	1 each
Dijon Mustard	½ cup
Yellow Mustard	¼ cup
Corn Syrup	½ cup
Molasses	2 tablespoons
Black Pepper, ground	½ teaspoon
Salt	½ teaspoon

Preparation

1. Combine all the ingredients in a heavy sauce pan and bring to a boil over medium high heat.

2. Reduce heat and simmer until thick, about 15 – 20 minutes. Transfer to a plastic container, cool and then refrigerate.

Grilling Juice

Put this into a squeeze bottle or just brush onto meats and fish as they are grilling. This is not a marinade or sauce it is used to keep the item moist while cooking.

Ingredients

Soy Sauce	½ cup
Red Wine, dry	¼ cup
Cider Vinegar	¼ cup

Preparation

1. Mix everything together in a bowl, transfer to a plastic container or a squirt bottle. Refrigerate until ready to use.

Steak Butter

Spread a small amount onto steaks or other meats as they finish cooking before transferring to a serving platter.

Ingredients

Butter, room temperature	1 cup
A.1. Steak Sauce	¼ cup
Parsley, chopped	1 tablespoon

Preparation

1. Place the butter in a bowl and whip using an electric mixer until light and fluffy.

2. Add the steak sauce and parley and mix well. Cover and refrigerate. Leave out at room temperature for an hour before using.

Lemon Aioli

This is especially nice with any kind of fried fish or put it on a sandwich.

Ingredients

Lemon, juiced	3 each
Garlic, chopped	1 clove
Turmeric	⅛ teaspoon
Mayonnaise	1 cup
Dill, chopped	2 teaspoons
Salt and White Pepper	as needed

Preparation

1. Place the lemon juice, garlic and turmeric in a blender and puree until smooth. Pour into a pan and bring to a simmer over medium high heat. Reduce heat and simmer until about two tablespoons of juice remain. Remove from heat and pour into a bowl, let cool.

2. Add the rest of the ingredients to the bowl and whisk until smooth and there are no remaining lumps of mayonnaise. Cover and refrigerate at least one hour before serving.

Chili Aioli

An Asian twist on an old favorite but it works well with lots of stuff and has a good balance between sweet and spicy.

Ingredients

Mayonnaise	1 cup
Chili Sauce, sriracha brand	⅓ cup
Sesame Oil	1 tablespoon
Sugar	2 teaspoons
Green Onion, white part only, chopped	2 teaspoons
Pickled Ginger, chopped	2 teaspoons

Preparation

1. In a mixing bowl whisk together the mayonnaise and chili sauce until smooth and there are no remaining lumps of mayonnaise.

2. Add all of the remaining ingredients and mix well. Cover and refrigerate at least one hour before serving.

Sweet and Sour Sauce

This has a great flavor and various uses but to make it look like what is served at the local restaurant you may want to add a few drops of red food coloring at the very end.

Ingredients

Rice Vinegar	⅔ cup
Pineapple Juice	½ cup
Ketchup	½ cup
Sugar	½ cup
Fresh Ginger, chopped	1 tablespoon
Garlic, chopped	1 tablespoon
Green Onion, white part only, chopped	1 tablespoon
Chili Sauce, Sriracha	1 teaspoon
Cornstarch	4 teaspoons
Chicken Stock	2 tablespoons

Preparation

1. In a heavy sauce pot boil the vinegar, pineapple juice, ketchup, sugar, ginger, garlic, green onion and chili sauce. Reduce heat and simmer for 5 minutes, pour into a blender and puree until smooth. Return to the pot and bring back to a boil.

2. Whisk together the cornstarch and chicken stock in a small bowl. Slowly pour into the sauce while constantly stirring. Simmer for 2 minutes, remove from heat and allow to cool before refrigerating.

Cocktail Sauce

A must have for any type of cold seafood, adjust the amount of horseradish if you prefer yours with a bigger kick.

Ingredients

Ketchup	1 cup
Prepared Horseradish	2 tablespoons
Lemon Juice	2 tablespoons
Worcestershire Sauce	1 tablespoon
Fresh Dill, chopped	2 teaspoons
Tabasco Sauce	¼ teaspoon

Preparation

1. In a large bowl mix together all of the ingredients. Cover and refrigerate for at least an hour before using.

Tartar Sauce

Ingredients

Mayonnaise	1 cup
Dill Pickle, chopped	¼ cup
Green onion, chopped	3 tablespoons
Capers, drained and chopped	4 teaspoons
Parsley, chopped	1 tablespoon
Lemon, juiced	½ each
Dijon mustard	1 teaspoon
Dill, chopped	2 teaspoons
Tabasco Sauce	¼ teaspoon

Preparation

1. In a large bowl mix together all of the ingredients. Cover and refrigerate for at least an hour before using.

Seasoned Oyster Crackers

Ingredients

Oyster Crackers	2 cups
Butter, melted	¼ cup
Salt	1 teaspoon
Garlic Powder	1 teaspoon
Dill, dried	1 teaspoon
White Pepper	½ teaspoon

Preparation

1. Preheat oven to 350°.

2. Place the crackers in a bowl and drizzle with the butter. Add the remaining ingredients and gently stir until the crackers are evenly seasoned.

3. Pour onto a baking sheet and spread into one even layer. Bake until lightly golden, stirring occasionally, about 8 – 10 minutes.

Venison Country Sausage

~This will make about 40 sausages

Ingredients

Venison, trimmed well	6 pounds
Boneless Pork Butt, diced	4 pounds
Sugar	4 tbsp
Kosher Salt	6 tbsp
Onion Powder	2 tbsp
Ground White Pepper	2 tsp
Hungarian Paprika	4 tsp
Pink Salt	2 tsp
Ground Allspice	1 tsp
Ground Nutmeg	1 tsp
Ground Black Pepper	2 tsp
Garlic Powder	1 tsp
Ice Water	2 cups

Preparation

1. Combine all of the ingredients except the water and toss to mix thoroughly, refrigerate until ready to grind.

2. Grind the mixture through the small die into a bowl set in ice.

3. Add the water and beat with the paddle attachment, or a sturdy wooden spoon, until the water is incorporated and the mixture develops a uniform, sticky appearance, about 1 minute on medium speed.

4. Cook and test a small piece if desired.

5. Stuff the sausage into hog casings and twist into 6" links. Hang and let dry at room temperature for 2 hours.

6. Hot smoke at 180° to an internal temperature of 150°, chill in ice water before refrigerating.

Beef Jerky

This is a good basic jerky recipe that can easily be adjusted to your liking, if you want it sweeter, more peppery, whatever you like just adjust it accordingly.

Ingredients

Beef Flank Steak	3 pounds
Soy Sauce	20 ounces
Teriyaki Sauce	20 ounces
Worcestershire Sauce	15 ounces
Cola Soda	12 ounces
Brown Sugar	1 cup
Liquid Smoke	¾ cup
Molasses	½ cup
Garlic Powder	¼ cup
Onion Powder	¼ cup
Black Pepper, ground	3 tablespoons
Paprika, sweet smoked	2 tablespoons
Bamboo Skewers, 12"	24 -30 each

Preparation

1. Trim the beef very well, removing all fat and sinew. Slice the meat into long strips about 1" wide and thinner than a ¼". If necessary place the meat in a pan and freeze until ice crystals appear on the surface, about 20 minutes, then slice.

2. Mix all of the remaining ingredients together for the marinade. Add the beef slices and mix well. Place in a plastic container with a tight fitting lid and refrigerate for three days, stirring the meat at least twice a day.

3. Drain the meat in a colander, and then put 6 pieces on each skewer by stabbing through the very tip of each slice. Spread the meat apart by about 1". Line the bottom of the oven with foil to create a drip pan that will catch all of the juices as the meat dries. Place the rack in the top third of the oven and place each skewer along the rack so that the meat hangs freely through the slots. Separate the pieces so that none are touching each other.

4. Set the oven temperature to 170°. Cook the meat for 4 – 6 hours, opening the door every half an hour to release any steam and moisture. The meat is done when it easily tears apart, but is not so dry that it crumbles. Remove from oven and take off of the skewers. Allow to cool completely before storing in an airtight container.

Dill Pickles

Ingredients

Pickling Cucumbers, ⅛" slices	3 pounds
White Onion, ⅛" slices	2 each
Canning Salt	½ cup
Alum	1 teaspoon
White Vinegar	1 quart
Water	2 cups
Dill Seed	¼ cup

Preparation

1. In a large bowl mix together all of the vegetables, canning salt, and alum. Place into a plastic container, covered, and let stand overnight in a cool place.

2. Drain the vegetables and rinse with cold running water.

3. Bring the vinegar, water and dill seed to a boil in a large pot. Remove from heat. Either pack the vegetables into jars and follow the normal procedure for canning, or simply put the vegetables in plastic containers and cover with the vinegar solution and refrigerate.

Grandma Verna's Bread and Butter Pickles

Ingredients

Pickling Cucumbers, ⅛" slices	6 quarts
White Onion, ⅛" slices	12 each
Red Pepper, ⅛" slices	2 each
Canning Salt	½ cup
Alum	2 teaspoons
White Vinegar	2 quarts
Sugar	2 quarts
Mustard Seed	½ cup
Turmeric	3 tablespoons

Preparation

1. In a large bowl mix together all of the vegetables, canning salt, and alum. Place into a plastic container, covered, and let stand overnight in a cool place.

2. Drain the vegetables and rinse with cold running water.

3. Bring the vinegar, sugar, mustard seed and turmeric to a boil in a large pot. Add the vegetables and simmer until the pickles are transparent, about ten minutes. Remove from heat. Either follow the normal procedure for canning, or simply cool and refrigerate the pickles.

Beef Marinade

Ingredients

Red Wine, dry	2 cup
Soy Sauce	1 cup
Limes, juiced	2 each
White Onion, thin slices	1 each
Garlic, chopped	¼ cup

Preparation

1. In a large bowl mix together and refrigerate until needed. Depending on what is being marinated you may prefer to strain out the vegetables first.

Index